KT-433-494

This book is to be returned on or before the last date stamped below.   728

LIBREX

The twentieth-century house

Laurence King
Publishing
in association with
Glasgow 1999

Deyan Sudjic
with Tulga Beyerle

The twentieth-century house

Home

Published 1999 by Laurence King
Publishing, London
in association with Glasgow 1999
Festival Company Ltd
Laurence King Publishing is an
imprint of Calmann & King Ltd
71 Great Russell Street
London WC1B 3BN
Tel: +44 171 831 6351
Fax: +44 171 831 8356
e-mail: enquiries@calmann-king.co.uk

A catalogue record for this book is
available from the British Library.

ISBN 1 85669 154 3

Designed by Esterson Lackersteen
Picture research by Suzanne Hodgart

Printed in Italy

Home: the twentieth-century house
Homes for the Future Site
Greendyke Street
Glasgow G1
1 July–31 October 1999

Glasgow 1999
Director: Deyan Sudjic
Depute Director: Eleanor McAllister
Curators: Deyan Sudjic and
Tulga Beyerle
Project Management: Richard
Greenwood Partnership
Exhibition Design: Esterson
Lackersteen, Atelier Works
Audio-visual: 55°
Exhibition Coordinator: Rock DCM
Site Design: Ben Kelly
Site Graphics: Paul Khera

Associate Sponsors

Glasgōw 1999
UK City of
Architecture
and Design

Contents

109328
728

Introduction

We are all of us fascinated by the house. By our own home, of course. It's the place in which we live, day after day, year after year. It gives us shelter and comfort, both physically and emotionally. It's where we retreat when we are ill, and it's the place in which we celebrate the major events of our lives. Even more fundamentally, it serves to define who we are, and who we are not. It's the place in which, until our grandparents' time, all of us were born, and where most of us would still prefer to be when we die. For those for whom owning a home is a recent phenomenon, its very existence forms the bedrock of security, as well, paradoxically, as causing considerable financial anxiety.

The continual reconfiguration of the home to cope with our changing needs – we get married, produce children, divorce, remarry, and grow older – shapes and celebrates our lives, and provides a physical memory of their course. Built on these practical and emotional needs, the house is also the focus of a rich fantasy life of hopes and dreams. Other people's houses are even more fascinating than our own. They are so endlessly revealing that they cannot help but appeal to all our most voyeuristic instincts.

We all have our own personal predilections that translate into those curious little individual tics of taste and style, expressed in everything from our choice of carpets, curtains and even plumbing, to furniture. Such ostensibly trivial details offer endless opportunities to indulge in the exhibitionism that is never far from the surface in any discussion of domestic architecture.

Our home is a reflection of the way that we see ourselves, or perhaps more accurately, of how we would like ourselves to be seen. The parallels with the clothes that we wear are obvious. There is both a functional issue to address, and an emotional one. Like our clothes, our houses are shaped both by convention, and also by the constant urge to transgress the conventions. Fashion is an issue both for clothes and for housing, as is technology and the availability of new materials.

There are other, more innocent, less narcissistic, but equally deep-rooted issues at work. We know what houses ought to be, and how they should look. Whatever our culture or background, we are all influenced by that moment in childhood when we first become aware of the doll's house picture of what the house is, and the symbolic power that it has on our imagination. For ever after, we share a communal memory that defines the notion of what a house is like. A pitched roof and a symmetrical pattern of windows around a door is part of the essential visual domestic landscape we all carry with us, even if we have never lived, and will never live in such a place. Inevitably, it is an image that sets the parameters for a discussion that defines the architecture of the house.

And then we are riveted by the idea of the house in the abstract: not by my house or your house, but the house. The house is at the intersection of most of the major issues that shape contemporary life. Its form is a reflection of our attitudes to the family, to social rituals, courtship, money, memory, class and gender. The way that housing is funded is nothing less

than the crystallization of an entire economic system. And the relationship of one house to another is a reflection of the most fundamental urban structures. The house defines the street and the neighbourhood, which in turn shapes the entire city. Its form and location governs our relationship with the world of work and of civic life. And it shapes our relationships with each other at a fundamental level. Is the home a place that is designed to be shared with an extended family? Is it a place that can allow social interaction to take place comfortably? Or is the standard house too small, and its location within the city too atomized for such activities – as is the case in contemporary Japan, for example, where most communal life takes place in the public realm (department stores, cafés, hotels and railway stations) rather than the private, domestic one?

Is the home a place in which people can earn their living? This was once the case in the eighteenth-century houses of Spitalfields in east London, where Huguenot weavers built themselves attic workshops, and is still common throughout Asia in the form of the 'shop house' where a family will live and work, protecting their investment, sleeping beneath the storeroom and on top of their street-level retail outlet.

The house tells us about the impact of technology on the domestic world, and it provides a unique insight into practically every other significant aspect of human life, from the way in which we keep ourselves clean, to the way in which we choose to tell the world how important we are. And while the fundamentals of shelter, emotional

1. Richard Rogers, writing in 1975 in *Architecture* magazine. See *Foster, Rogers and Stirling, New British Architecture*, Deyan Sudjic, London 1986.

support and memory remain constant, the aesthetic, spatial and technical issues continuously fluctuate. That fluctuation represents the social history of the twentieth century, which could perfectly well be told through a close examination of the house.

It is hardly surprising that the single-family house has occupied so much of the attention of so many architects. For most of this century, the house has been at the centre stage of architecture. Acting as a kind of lightning rod, it has served to distil the essence of successive waves of architectural invention. Yet to explore the subject of the design of the individual house at this particular point in the history of contemporary architecture demands a certain amount of justification. Despite its long and significant history, the single-family house has come to be seen by certain critics as an emblem of affluent irrelevance, not least in the view of some architects. They have found the design of the house continually fascinating, as well as the subject of endless ideological reservations. Richard Rogers's words on the subject of the individual house in the 1970s are telling: 'In an age of homelessness and mass starvation, the individual house, no matter how beautiful, is not the answer'.[1] This was written shortly after he and Norman Foster, in practice together as Team 4, designed Creak Vean, the remarkable house in Cornwall that launched both their careers. Not that this is by any means an original critique of the dilemma facing so many contemporary architects attempting to square the circle between social and aesthetic concerns. Collectivism and social housing have been a defining strand

of modernism since before the 1920s. The expansion of major Dutch and German cities between the two world wars, under the leadership of key modern movement figures such as J.J.P. Oud in Rotterdam and Ernst May in Frankfurt, made modern architecture synonymous with social housing. Yet among the pioneers were some architects who were ready to exploit any possibility to build, provided that it gave them the chance to realize their visions. It was an intellectual promiscuity that earned them the bitter criticism of their peers. When Ludwig Mies van der Rohe completed the Tugendhat house in Brno in 1931 for example, a strident strand of local architectural opinion took exactly the same view that Rogers was to express so many years later. The Czech critic Karel Teige described not just the house designed by Mies, but also works by Frank Lloyd Wright, Adolf Loos and Le Corbusier, as 'the ultimate in modern snobbery, and re-editions of the splendid baroque palace as a powerhouse for the financial nobility of our age'. Yet this was the same Mies van der Rohe who had been responsible for the master planning of the Wiessenhof Siedlung on the edges of Stuttgart which explored the design of innovative low-cost housing with such force that it was singled out by the Nazis for especially vehement condemnation as 'Arab Town', and was represented by them as the embodiment of cosmopolitan decadence.

In most of the world, commissioning an individual house has become an increasingly unsubtle display of wealth. The great stock market bull run of the 1990s left corporate America under the spell of Bill Gates, and carpeted with ever

larger and more ostentatious mansions. The destruction of perfectly serviceable homes by bigger and better examples became one of the more outrageous design phenomena of the period, as the newly wealthy, desperate to live in areas that reflected their own sense of self-worth, were ready to buy houses for the sake of their sites alone, pulling down whatever they found to make way for something newer.

The design of the individual house is based on a far closer relationship between the individual occupant and the architect than is now common for almost every other category of architectural commission. As a result, the fashionable domestic architect turned into a court jester for the affluent when they were enjoying the fruits of the boom years, as well as, in some instances, embarking on an unofficial relationship as counsellor, psychoanalyst and trophy. A similar process took shape in an even more extreme form in Russia after the collapse of the Soviet Union, with the rise of the kleptocracy and the ever more conspicuous dachas that they built for themselves from the proceeds of the pillaging of the old economic system. This is an area of design that is based on fantasies of grandeur, exaggerated modernity and exoticism, blended together surrealistically in a queasy mixture of kitsch and Freudian symbolism. Individuals can be alarmingly frank in the imagery they adopt for their own homes, though they tend to feed off each other: Southern plantations, Tudor cottages, Cotswold manor houses, Riviera villas and Spanish haciendas are universally popular in almost any

climate and context, provided cash is abundant. Today, millionaire's row in London, Moscow or Houston looks much the same: a collection of glossy ostentation, littered with porticoes and pediments, giant houses that are endlessly spreading their wings, covered swimming pools, exercise gyms and coach houses big enough for fleets of stretch limousines. Aesthetically, these houses are designed very much in the way of the burgeoning high-rises of South-East Asia, consuming architectural images at random and supplying electronically generated collages of fashionable motifs.

The critical reaction to these houses employs much the same terms that were used in the nineteenth century by the supporters of the Arts and Crafts movement in their excoriation of the vulgar ignorance of the nouveau riche industrialists who poured their fortunes into swaggering, bombastic mansions. But the image of the architect-designed house still continues to percolate through into the wider market, just as couture fashion defines high-street style. Many of the most extreme and bizarre specimens clustered along Bishop's Avenue in London, or in Post Oak around the Galleria in Houston, base their flamboyant invention on a language of design defined by supposedly critically respectable architects. And while the high-minded architectural professionals who claim to speak for the masses are sincere in their belief that the single house is of no practical use, there is enormous popular interest in how the house looks, and even more in using the home to define a sense of individualism.

The gulf between the extreme flamboyance of contemporary one of a kind houses, of architectural tastes, and the norms of social housing is by no means as wide as some critics would claim. Social housing that has been sold to its tenants instantly begins to sprout the most obvious signs of militant individualism, from wagon wheels on the fence, to stone cladding on the walls and satellite dishes on the roof. In the same way, the motifs of the high-design world percolate into the compounds of the rich.

And yet the story of the first 30 years of the twentieth century could be told almost entirely through a series of extraordinarily refined individual houses. Beyond that, for perhaps the first half of the twentieth century, contemporary architecture could still be measured out in terms of a judicious selection of houses that embodied the values of architectural culture. An unbroken sequence stretched from Otto Wagner to Adolf Loos, and from Mies van der Rohe to Eileen Gray and Charles and Ray Eames. That succession is much harder to trace now. Perhaps it is because we are too close to judge the lasting merit of individual examples of domestic architecture. Or just possibly, as a means of cultural expression, the individual house is in danger of going the same way as portrait painting, reduced to a faint and irrelevant provincial echo of a once distinguished art form. Perhaps it is because the reality of the way we live our lives now means that houses do not offer the scope to be as interesting as they once were. Perhaps, like contemporary art, there is room only for one Picasso and one Duchamp in any century, and everything else is simply an

ever more mechanical repetition. Has there ever really been anything of the same intensity as the house that Gerrit Rietveld built for Truus Schröder-Schräder in Utrecht shortly after the First World War, still less a house that has been endowed with such power in the last ten years? Is the recent domestic work of Frank Gehry or Rem Koolhaas really of a significance equivalent to the early villas of Le Corbusier? And yet houses go on being designed and built. They are still the most interesting work of many architects. They are the starting point of many architectural careers, and they serve as agenda-setting landmarks. They are the test beds for experimentation in style and technique. They are calling cards and manifestos.

The house is a complicated, highly charged part of the architectural landscape, in which high art and popular culture come together in a head-on collision. Back in the 1920s, Willy Baumeister designed a poster that laid bare all the fears and antagonisms between architectural taste and conventional notions of comfort and propriety. To advertise the housing exhibition that formed part of Mies van der Rohe's Weissenhof Siedlung in Stuttgart in the summer of 1927, Baumeister chose to draw attention to the experimental interiors on show produced by a group of avant-garde designers from all over Europe with a black-and-white photograph of a traditional interior full of heavy furniture and antimacassars, brutally cancelled out in splashy red paint, with the question 'how should we live?' scrawled across it. The answer was clearly calculated to bring little comfort to people who did not live in glass houses.

Houses are shaped by architects

spurred by a sense of mission, but also by the forces of naked consumerism. Some are the result of a production line, as if they were an industrially made consumer item, with the same plan and the same elevations repeated all over the country, though they are styled with a lack of subtlety that would be inconceivable in the car industry. People want their house to say something about them. To show to the world how much money they have made, or how long it has been since their ancestors made it for them. Or else, to demonstrate just how much culture and learning they have acquired. They use houses to show how much self-confidence they have, or how fashionable they are, or even what a happy marriage they have. People build new houses in the optimistic belief that they make possible a new way of life. And architects go on searching for ways of defining these beliefs in new ways.

New houses are constructed to impress friends, and to accommodate possessions. We build for the sake of building. Construct one house, and the chances are that you will do it again. House building becomes an end in itself. Which means that having built once, you move, and move again. You move even if you are William Morris, abandoning a unique creation, such as the Red House. You move even if you are Eileen Gray, leaving the single most important creation of your career to the less than tender mercy of Graham Sutherland, the English artist who left his unsympathetic mark on her pristine house. People move more and more often. At the end of the twentieth century, Americans sell up and relocate as

often as once in every three years. The British are catching up rapidly. We are mobile in the extreme. We move before we have the time to accumulate the detritus of possessions that we use to define ourselves. As we change things, walls move back and forth. Windows are inserted and blocked up, and then reopened again. Environmental controls are constantly upgraded. Extensions are added and subtracted. The affluent use an interior decorator to equip themselves with the appropriate patina of memories and traditions that serve to reflect their aspirations.

A house is not only about architectural design. It is, or can be, about decoration. It is defined more and more by the burgeoning quantity of domestic objects that are taking an increasingly foreground role in the domestic interior. But beyond those issues, we are interested in houses as voyeurs as well as social explorers. We are fascinated, in spite of ourselves, by other people's homes: they tell us about the lives of their inhabitants and despite efforts to present a carefully selected view, they almost always succeed in presenting a dazzlingly frank reflection of the actual values of their owners, rather than the image that their architects hope they will project. Yet while the architectural profession has continued to shape the continuing evolution of the house, architects have rarely acknowledged the wider aspects of the meaning of the home.

1900–1999: The history of the domestic idea

1

The end of tradition

1900–1910

The portrayal of the modern movement – twentieth-century architecture's troublesome teenage phase – as a once-and-for-all break with the past used to be an essential part of the apparatus of conventional architectural history. The modern movement was represented as being just as decisive in its own way as the slightly earlier break with representational art triggered by photography.

As far as architecture is concerned, modernity was supposedly the end of tradition. It was defined as a deliberate and necessary rupture, represented by its partisans as a virtue that offered a positive alternative to the stagnation of continuity. Modernity was presented as not just a reflection of changing functional issues and new materials, but also as the embodiment of a new sensibility. Rather than being rooted in the repetition and refinement of familiar forms, as it had allegedly been for a thousand years, domestic architecture in the early part of this century became fixated by originality for its own sake.

The modern house was a battering ram, used by the early moderns as part of their onslaught on conventional ideas – if not necessarily on how domestic life should be lived, then certainly on how it should look. White walls, unadorned ceilings and glazed walls were in themselves an emblem of newness. As familiarity made even the most extreme ideas routine, shock tactics had constantly to be reinforced and pushed to new limits, if they were to remain effective.

But initially at least, the rapidly changing shape of the modern house was a phenomenon that was of relevance only to the tiny segment of the population of western Europe and America that enjoyed a sufficient degree of affluence. Among them, it was an even narrower slice of that segment who had the social confidence to use their affluence to make a home that avoided the obvious trappings of conventional status. For the great majority of the urban population at the beginning of the nineteenth century, the notion of living in an individual house of any kind was as alien as the prospect of an indoor lavatory, or a bathroom. For most people, home was a tenement. In London, such dwellings were described, by commentators such as Charles Dickens, as rookeries: urban catacombs in which an entire family might share a single room with nothing more than an oblique view of daylight, surrounded on every side by neighbours in similar circumstances. In Berlin, Chicago or Glasgow, conditions were little different. In all of these cities, a dense core of tenement blocks six or seven storeys high defined the urban context. It was a housing type not that much different from those that shaped ancient Rome.

For the better-off working and middle classes in nineteenth-century England, there was a range of terraced houses available – carefully graded in size and quality according to the budget of the relevant household. But these houses addressed only a certain strand of the potential market. Houses for the truly affluent generally did their best to recreate the rural model in an urban context. In a few of the great urban set pieces – John Nash's Regent's Park or the Edinburgh New Town – such houses were grouped together to suggest a palatial scale.

Despite a great deal of violent rhetoric, the rupture with history did not come all at once. Indeed, the first effective voice of dissent advocated a revolution that looked backward rather than forward. William Morris was a highly effective propagandist in word and deed for the most jaundiced possible view of industrial civilization. As Morris saw it, the machine had produced a culture so base and degraded that the only honourable course left was to destroy it, and rebuild a mythical version of the Middle Ages in its place.

Morris's new world order was focused on the home. And it was as a decorator, with his natural gift for the pattern-making detail of wallpaper, that he was most successful. With its free-form improvisation on manorial themes, the Red House, on the outer suburban fringes of London and designed for the young Morris by Philip Webb in 1859, gave a clue as to what his homespun alternative to the industrial world might look like. Much later, in *News from Nowhere* (1890), an older, more radical Morris provided a literary account of what life would be like in this post-industrial utopia and how it might be achieved. The city, and the centralized state that had produced it, would wither away, to be replaced by anarchic, dispersed, self-sufficiency. The Red House was a halting, stumbling vision of what a house could be in such circumstances. It combined an intellectual view of the potential of domestic architecture to express an ideology with enough crowd-pleasing popular appeal to become an aspirational consumerist dream – not that these two facets of domesticity are by any means

William Morris
commissioned Philip
Webb to design the
neo-medieval Red House
in 1859 (top), setting
the scene for a much

freer Arts and
Crafts movement, as
demonstrated by C.F.A.
Voysey's Broadleys in
Cumbria, north-west
England, of 1898 (below).

1. See Fiona MacCarthy's
biography, *William
Morris*, London 1995.

antithetical. A house that looked as if it was rooted in its landscape, and which could evoke memories of a golden age, was one that appealed to the self-image of a newly affluent class. The warm red-brick facades, picturesque turreted roofs and a simplified, relatively austere interior may have appeared to represent a break with conventional bourgeois solidity, but they were also immediately associated with a sense of comfort and ease almost as rapidly as Morris's stylized floral wallpaper won the hearts of Britain's middle classes. They represented the promise that lasting values were still attainable, even in the midst of an avalanche of social change. It was an image which was quickly communicated in the field of mass housing as well. Early attempts to improve the condition of the working classes in London were based on apartment buildings that took their form from the Arts and Crafts movement. The very architects who were in most demand by the progressive bourgeoisie to design their houses were those who were interested enough in social change to become involved with housing for the deserving poor.

The image of the single-family house as a sought-after ideal was a reaction against the industrial world. It was a domestic idyll, a promise of salvation through the redemption of the family. And in turn, it was this individualist ideal that the machine age housing of the 1920s reacted against, with its counter-dream of a collectivist future.

From its Anglo-Saxon origins, this architectural vocabulary of domesticity quickly spread around Europe, in part through the

propaganda efforts of Hermann Muthesius, the German architect attached to the Kaiser's embassy in London at the turn of the century. His influential book, *Das englische Haus*, of 1904, reproduced many of the pioneering architectural works of the period and attracted huge interest throughout the Continent. Indeed, Muthesius projected not just an architectural vocabulary, but a philosophical approach to design as well, which, much like Adolf Loos, identified the England of 1900 as the international focus of modernity. Muthesius claimed that the English were not interested in 'show or comfort' in the kitchen because 'middle-class housewives never cross its threshold', unlike their German counterparts who regarded 'the kitchen as [their] concern and arrange it lovingly throughout'.

If an Arts and Crafts house at the start of the twentieth century held the same relation to a classical villa from the late-nineteenth century as a home-made dress to an evening gown, the process of cultural confrontation went much further in the decades that followed. The design of houses in this period reflects a continuing sense of tension between designer and patron – a conflict that William Morris had enthusiastically embraced with his famous plea to the heavens to be freed from the necessity of 'pandering to the swinish luxury of the idle rich'.[1] It is notable how many of the most culturally ambitious individual houses of this period were either designed by architects for their own use, or for exceptional individuals – such as the art-dealing Steins, who were not only close to Picasso, but who also commissioned Le Corbusier to design a house for them on the outskirts of Paris.

More recently, it has become an equally orthodox view that the break with tradition was never as final as all that. In the 1970s, a new generation of critics looked at Le Corbusier's houses and discovered in them not just a blueprint of the machine for living in, as advertised by its inventor, but also the facade geometry of a Palladian villa, as well as the structural vaults of a Catalan farmhouse, while others identified a classical underpinning to the reductionist aesthetics of Ludwig Mies van der Rohe.

Instead of a revolution at the start of this century, we are now presented with a different script to account for this period, based on the notion of continuity. According to this view, the moderns were not iconoclasts at all, but actually maintained an interest in certain fundamental architectural qualities. Nor is modernity tied any longer to the twentieth century: the Age of Enlightenment is commonly presented as the start of modernity. According to this view, all the intellectual arguments for functionalism, truth to materials and simplicity had already been formulated long before the 1920s.

Today, no one denies that the aesthetic strands shaping architectural development during the first half of the twentieth century embraced a far richer range of expression than that allowed for in simplistic and highly partisan contemporary accounts. We are now in a position to take a more inclusive view. The champions of one tendency no longer feel the need to fight their corners with quite such vehemence as they once did. Edwin Lutyens and Le Corbusier, together with Otto Wagner and Alvar Aalto managed

to share a world stage, though they might have had very little to say to each other. Yet in one way or another, they all managed to engage with the historical language of architecture, even as they modified it to their own quite different ends. And all of them were able to present their ideas in the most distilled way through the single-family house. This process could be seen in the complex motivations of an exceptional architect such as Otto Wagner, in whose career a variety of creative impulses can be seen, ranging from what is conventionally described as eclecticism, to modernity. Individuals shift in their views. And their work acquires different meanings as time goes by. Look at the remarkable phenomenon that has turned once revolutionary houses into museum pieces, sacred fragments of architectural heritage, protected like holy relics, yet paradoxically stripped of all their original meaning. It is striking how long it took many architects to discover the means of breaking finally with the past. Both Le Corbusier and Mies van der Rohe began their careers working in a transitional idiom. In La Chaux-de-Fonds, Le Corbusier's Swiss birthplace, his earliest architectural works were rooted in a struggle to produce a regional architecture arising from a distinctive sense of place, and based on devising a system of expressive ornament. Mies's early houses were equally distanced from his mature work. He began as an overt classicist, as is to be expected from an architect who started his career in the office of Peter Behrens. Historicism can coexist with the demonstrative incorporation of technologically

based architectural features. The search for national identity does not exclude an architecture rooted in the poetry of pure space. All of these are concepts that have been embodied in individual houses. At the same time, it is clear that even the prelude to the modern movement was never the monolithic aesthetic expression that it was once represented as being, but was full of dissent and fractures and conflict. When Adolf Loos denounced ornament as crime, it was not vulgar nineteenth-century eclecticism he had in his sights, but his own Viennese Secessionist contemporaries.

Despite the fluctuations of intellectual fashion, it is clear that something quite decisive and radical really did overtake architecture in the early years of the twentieth century. The question is: exactly what was that something? In part, the answer is the impact of an avalanche of technical innovation. William Morris died too soon to have to confront the invasion of the modern domestic realm by electricity, and still less to be forced to make a considered aesthetic response to it, but his enthusiasm for the Middle Ages does not seem to have extended as far as refusing to accept a water-borne sewage disposal system in his own home.

Victor Horta, Charles Rennie Mackintosh and Frank Lloyd Wright built their first major houses within 20 years of the commissioning by Swan and Edison of the first commercial electric power stations in London and New York. All of them used electricity to light their houses at a time when it was still an unusual source of illumination, and all of them embraced modern plumbing. In themselves these were both deliberate and easily

understood signals of their modernity. And while it is naive to believe, as some of the more literal-minded members of the modern movement once did, that such technical innovations were the determinants of a new architecture, there can be no doubt that even on a simple pragmatic level, they had a radical impact on the process of designing a house. Electric light for example had the effect of transforming the spatial quality of the interior. Over several centuries the design of the light fitting had been tailored to particular sources of light: once oil and candles, later gas. And these unsteady, flickering incandescent flames were multiplied and enhanced by cut-glass chandeliers, multifaceted reflectors that would give a very specific quality to the light, and would shape the visual perception of an interior by its occupants. Electricity altered all that. It also had the immediate effect of challenging architects, designers and engineers to consider what form the modern light fitting should take. Was electric light going to adopt the outward shape of a candle, just as the first internal combustion-powered automobiles were literally horseless carriages? Electric light was a clean light source. For the first time, there were no products of combustion, so that white became a sensible option as a colour for the domestic interior. But the results went further. The design of the contents of the living room – its furniture, glass and tableware – had formed a kind of partnership, adapted for the way in which candlelight could be reflected in their facets, and designed so that points of light could be set dancing in them.

Edwin Lutyens's domestic work was viewed by unsympathetic critics as representing a historical dead end. Yet houses such as Castle Drogo, Devon, of 1910–30 (top) and Tigbourne Court, Surrey, of 1899 (below), were no less inventive than Mackintosh's designs.

Electric light changed that relationship forever. Electricity was spreading rapidly as a network of power stations were constructed around the developed world, but even as late as 1902, just eight per cent of American homes had a main electricity supply. Final proof that disease was spread by germs was just as recent a discovery. And it was an understanding that was to have an equally significant impact on the form of houses, and their layout inside and out.

As building materials, iron was 100 years old, steel no more than 20 and aluminium just a decade. They still had to become visible in the domestic context, beyond the greenhouse and the conservatory, though their potential was already clear. Massive walls, and the traditionally cellular layout of the house – one cave-like space opening into another – was no longer necessary. The heating system was also put to work in new ways: it was no longer necessary to huddle around an open fire as ducted air and hot-water radiators allowed much more of the floor area of the house to be put to use, just as electric light expanded the usable area of the house after dark.

It was impossible for architects to ignore the pressure to find an appropriate means of accommodating and expressing the extent of the transformation ushered in by these developments. Indeed, it had been the recurring theme of nineteenth-century critical architectural thought. At the same time, cultural nationalism was asserting itself. An expanding urban middle class, affluent enough to afford servants, had emerged and they were enjoying the beginning of a torrent of consumer goods.

Gradually, the balance of power between the house and its contents began to shift decisively in favour of the latter. With the growth of industrialized production, it was noticeable that furniture, lighting, cutlery and household appliances began to be purchased ready made, rather than purpose designed and manufactured to order by specialist craftsmen. And their value began to account for an increasing proportion of the budget for constructing and equipping a new house. Architects, almost without being aware of what was happening, were beginning to defer to industrial design. But the process did not happen all at once, and the defining houses of the first decade of the twentieth century were designed to accommodate a way of life that had changed little from that of the nineteenth century. New houses were typically built for successful businessmen, who would use the railway or the tram to reach their office every day. Their wives did not work and the household had a full complement of servants who lived on the premises.

Despite all this continuity, the language of architectural debate at the beginning of the twentieth century became increasingly inflammatory. Victor Horta was far from being the most provocative of the voices proselytizing for a new architectural order at this point. Quite the contrary. He was among the most accomplished exponents of Art Nouveau in its Belgian heartland, and Art Nouveau now seems a seductive – much more than a confrontational – movement. Compared to an authentic iconoclast, a futurist like F.T. Marinetti say, who was prepared to celebrate the poetry of crowds, railway stations and even war,

2. Frank Lloyd Wright, *In the Cause of Architecture*, first published in *Architectural Record*, 1908. Reproduced in C.R. Ashbee's introduction to volume 2 of the Wasmuth edition on Wright.

3. *Ornament and Crime*, originally published as a newspaper article in 1908, appeared in Loos's collected essays, *Trotzdem*, in 1931. The essay appears in English in L. Munz and G. Kunstler's *Adolf Loos, Pioneer of Modern Architecture*, 1966.

Horta's work was gentleness itself in its attempt to create naturally occurring forms in new materials. And yet even an architect of his disposition did not shrink from revolutionary rhetoric. Horta began his architectural career under the influence of Alphonse Balat, a classicist who was responsible for many of the landmarks taking shape in the new Brussels at the end of the nineteenth century. Horta spelt out in the clearest possible language the exact nature of the break with the past that he was looking for. He wrote of his teacher Balat's aesthetic paralysis:

'His works are masterpieces of their kind, yet he never dared to abandon traditional forms. Only when he came to use iron, a material the Greeks had never used, was he able to follow his personal inspiration. Seeing the flight of this powerful intelligence hampered by the memory of forms from the past, I felt a revolt stirring in me, and resolved to try something else, to give life loyally and sincerely to the forms that welled up in my imagination.'

Certainly, Horta – like many of his contemporaries – revelled in originality for the sake of originality. In the mansions that he designed for his bourgeois clients, as well as his own house in Brussels, he used materials entirely unfamiliar to the domestic context in a way that could be seen as deliberately provocative. It was as if he had something to prove, as indeed he did. The materials he used for his interiors – bare brick and cast iron – on show as the primary means of architectural expression (whiplash patterns colliding with moulded cornices, stencil-patterned walls and multicoloured glass) are certainly

determinedly of their time. Horta created a tension between the solid massiveness of stone and sinuously attenuated metal.

Even the electric light fittings, mysteriously transformed into flowers with glass petals, are conspicuous in their frankness.

Horta refused to design facades that obeyed traditional notions of propriety: metal and glass were used in a way that appeared to flaunt structural logic, and yet they were clearly based on certain compositional conventions, acknowledged as much in their breach as in their observance. But behind his distinctive, idiosyncratic elevations and his lush plans, Horta's houses are deeply conventional in their reflection of social relations – as were so many of the supposedly revolutionary icons of domestic architecture at this moment.

At the start of the twentieth-century, from Vienna to Chicago, a variety of architects were looking for new means of expression for a variety of reasons. It was clear that these architects would have to formulate ways to deal with a wide range of additions to their repertoire, both in terms of building type and materials. Given that John Ruskin believed that exposed ironwork and architecture were mutually incompatible concepts, there was a pressing need for the development of a more relevant critical theory. Eugène-Emanuel Viollet-le-Duc's great treatise of the 1860s and 1870s, *Entretiens sur l'architecture*, was a useful pointer towards an approach to design appropriate to iron and glass.

In America, Frank Lloyd Wright, emerging from Louis Sullivan's office, and given a kick-start in his early career by Chicago's epic

building boom, was determined to invent his own architecture: 'The old structural forms which up to the present time have spelled "architecture" are decayed. Their life went from them long ago and new conditions, steel and concrete and terracotta in particular are prophesying a more plastic art wherein as the flesh is to our bones, so will the covering be to the structure', he wrote.[2]

Even in his early houses, Wright demonstrated a remarkable spatial fluidity, and he began to attract clients who wanted houses that were planned as unconventionally as they looked. There was an element of the exotic, and in particular, the influence of Japan, in his early houses, the product in part of Wright's exposure to a replica Japanese temple at the Chicago Colombian Exposition. Given the explosive nature of the growth of Chicago, and the number of recently wealthy clients wanting to build new houses for themselves, it is not surprising that Wright was able to secure more latitude in his work than many of his European contemporaries. Though of course, Wright was just as determined to impose his will on his clients as any of the European avant garde. He was determined to design every detail in the houses he built for his clients. Wright was bitterly disappointed not to have been able to design his own special telephones for the Larkin building in Buffalo, and could not be left alone in a room by a client without starting to rearrange the furniture to his own specifications.

But there was also a belief among other designers that a new way of life demanded new means of architectural expression. It is

clear in the writings of Adolf Loos for example that domestic architecture was not to be regarded as just a pragmatic, functional, or even picturesque issue. In Loos's view, the architect had a responsibility to pursue design with intellectual rigour and moral discipline. He thundered:

'We go to Beethoven or *Tristran* after the cares of the day. My shoemaker can't. I must not take away his joy as I have nothing to replace it with. But whoever goes to the Ninth Symphony and then sits down to design wallpaper is either a rogue or a degenerate.'[3]

Loos was taking such passionate objection not so much to the eclecticism of the nineteenth century, but to the much closer target of the Secessionists. He argued for purity as the only legitimate response of modern civilization to the industrial world. For Loos, the form of the house was a reflection of a whole set of moral and intellectual values: architects struggling to come to terms with modernity could do no other than attempt to address them.

Many of the individuals who patronized this generation of architects, despite the sometimes very traditional basis of their wealth, subscribed to this view. While it is Loos's individual houses that are his best-known works, he had an important input into the social housing of Vienna, despite his apparent dependence on luxurious materials. And yet the individual highlights of the domestic architecture of 1900 to 1910 must be described as being in transition – even to those temperamentally predisposed to doubt the very concept of progress from one idea to another. This was

an architectural moment that was still awaiting a resolution. The idea of a machine-age culture had yet to be fully translated into architectural form. And domestic paraphernalia, from the tap to the electrical system, had yet to assume a definitive shape. But this was also the moment at which the Viennese manufacturers were beginning to adapt their production lines to the new aesthetics of the moment. Instead of lifeless mechanical ornament and vulgar eclecticism, it was now possible to find Josef Hoffmann's highly refined designs for glassware on sale in Lobmeyer's store in Vienna. A modern furniture industry had already been created in Austria by Michael Thonet, who superseded the workshop's craft tradition with his network of factories scattered around the Austro-Hungarian empire, producing bentwood chairs and tables in their hundreds of thousands by using steam-formed standardized components. Thonet had produced the No. 14 bentwood chair in 1855. Until then furniture had been very much a matter of handicraft, depending on the production of very small batches of objects that were tailored to the needs of specific clients. Thonet's manufacturing process changed the status of furniture as being a precious item that would often be handed from generation to generation. By deskilling furniture manufacturing and investing in steam-bending techniques that could turn out millions of chairs, Thonet did for furniture what Henry Ford did for the motor car.

Peter Behrens – the architect who created the identity for the Allgemeine Elektrizitäts-Gesellschaft (AEG) and produced a range of completely new categories

of product – was the first industrial designer in the modern sense. AEG was originally the German licensee of Thomas Edison from 1907, a company that not only generated electrical power, but looked for ways to sell as much of it as it could. It sold electricity, as well as the household appliances that would consume increasing quantities of power. And it deliberately created an aesthetic sense that underscored the ideology of its products.

Behrens had spent four years in the artistic colony of Darmstadt, close to Frankfurt, where he made the transition from an early career as a painter to working as an architect and a designer. Behrens built himself a house while he was in Darmstadt that pushed the language of classical architecture to beyond breaking point and put him on the right side of the divide between tradition and innovation.

Edwin Lutyens, on the other hand, had the historical misfortune to be represented as the architect who more than any other was the embodiment of the end of a cultural epoch, rather than a pioneer at the beginning of one. Lutyens's remarkable houses were presented by unsympathetic critics in the 1950s as being built for the out-of-time aristocracy ready to be swept away by the catastrophe of the First World War. And yet, by any objective standards, these houses were of great architectural sophistication. Certainly, they were designed for clients who were no more reactionary than Charles Rennie Mackintosh's clients. What is there to distinguish the fantasy of Lutyens's Castle Drogo, built for a successful grocer, with Mackintosh's almost equally baronial Hill House, built for a successful publisher?

And Lutyens's houses were to prove a model for the masses. The ribbon development that spread like wildfire around cities stood in the same relationship to Lutyens's houses as high-street versions of ready-to-wear clothes do to the couture collections. Not so well made perhaps, and lacking subtlety and sophistication in planning and materials, but still recognizably from the same root.

Critical accounts of architectural development were once couched almost entirely in art-historical terms. But such an account missed the other meanings of the succession of single-family houses that serve to trace the development of architecture. Instead of examining the way in which such houses both reflected and shaped domestic life, the focus was all on the way in which a window was fitted into a facade. There is now much more interest in examining the other meanings of such designs: the insight they provide into relationships between men and women, as well as the way in which technology and mobility have redefined the meaning of domesticity with ever-increasing speed.

Cultural concerns have always been a driving force in domestic architectural developments. Horta came to prominence at a time when he and other architects of his generation were trying to define the idea of Belgium, just as Antoni Gaudí was designing the embodiment of a Catalan renaissance, and Mackintosh looked to shape a sense of modern Scotland. But individual houses are of course more than an abstraction of identity or a representation of narrowly architectural ideas. They are a very

Victor Horta was determined to create an aesthetic that made use of the material qualities of iron to the full, rather than concealing it within masonry. His starting point was an interest in sinuous, organic forms.

Horta's facade broke with Brussells' conventional classical street patterns, but it was the interior, with its extensive use of iron and glass, that expressed his inventive talent to the maximum.

floor plan

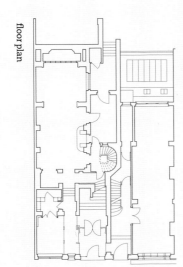

physical representation of identity. In this sense, many of the houses from the first years of the twentieth century, despite their restless aesthetic innovation, embody highly traditional social relationships. In such houses, parents were still insulated from children: accommodation that was manifestly inferior to the 'upstairs' world was provided for a range of downstairs servants. And in this context it should be understood that kitchens and laundries were the preserve of servants, not their masters. And very often, the kitchen was still a place that processed, as well as prepared, food for the table. It allowed the household to function without the retailer, baking bread, brewing beer and making butter and cheese. Contrast this with the position at the end of the twentieth century, when the kitchen has become not just part of the upstairs world of the master, but symbolically the very centre of even the wealthiest of homes. Marie Antoinette is no longer playing at being shepherdess, but at being cook. The successful housewife at the start of the century had to know how to find and keep a good cook. Now the job description is redundant. Middle-class women must learn how to bake bread like Tuscan peasants if they are to conform to the norms of metropolitan life. And they are expected to find personal fulfilment in assembling the ingredients from the hypermarket and the boutique grocer, rather than from the kitchen garden. At the same point in time, the sanitary aspects of the domestic interior were also in transition. Cleanliness and hygiene, regular bathing and water closets were becoming steadily more common, and the equipment involved was

being transformed from items of loose furniture into part of the architectural fabric.

The architectural profession itself was only just getting used to the idea of professional organization and limiting the profession to those with academic qualifications. Meanwhile, the engineers – who had also begun to organize themselves into a profession – began to emerge as a commercial challenge. While architects began to embrace functionalism, nobody could be more functional than the engineer, so just what exactly was left for the architect? At the same time, the house was becoming a commercial commodity, no longer tailor made, but more and more built and sold as a ready-made. For such commercial operations, the styling of the home became increasingly significant. The look of a house was starting to express itself in terms of an increasingly explicit social language. Indeed, it was an essential part of the marketing strategy of house builders. Certain details were used as the explicit signifiers of comfort, status and continuity.

Exactly where a house is built is determined by the wealth of its owner, and by his or her personal predilections. And of course also by the context of the time at which it is built. Until the suburban railways of the nineteenth century and the introduction of the season ticket, the physical extent of the world's great cities was limited by the endurance of pedestrians. The result was high-density urban settlement in which single-family houses were rare. Those very few who could afford it would build in a rural setting: the dwelling would be reached by horse, carriage, or occasionally, by boat. For the rest, it was high-density

urban living which shaped most of the world's cities until the middle of the nineteenth century. Horse-drawn trams, ducted pure water, sewage treatment systems and accessible electric power reshaped the context of the urban domestic world. For a brief moment, they made single-family urban houses available for a much larger number of people than had ever been previously possible. This dream, endlessly repeated, created the suburb, much to the alarm of the urban intellectuals. Le Corbusier's vision of high-density urbanism was one response; the Garden City movement was the other.

Horse-drawn trams were replaced by electric-powered trams from 1874 onward. Gas street lighting, introduced in London in 1807, gave way to electricity within a couple of generations. At the turn of the century, the individual house was caught between two worlds. Established social hierarchies demanded certain things of the home – such as the relationship between served and servants, children and adults, visitors and family and man and wife – that were reflected in its spatial configuration. At the same time, the exploding nineteenth-century metropolis had created a quite different context for the home.

When Charles Rennie Mackintosh built Hill House at Helensburgh outside Glasgow in 1902, cholera – which had as much to do with the shape of the modern house as any innovation – had only very recently been tamed. And the issue of hygiene was to exert a continuing power over the architectural imagination, not surprisingly when disease could affect even the affluent. Only a

generation earlier, Mackintosh's great Glaswegian predecessor, Alexander Thomson, had lost several children to the disease.

Mackintosh was the product of Glasgow, a city at the crest of a roaring tide of industrial growth that had spanned 100 years and which had not yet abated, a city whose elite had few connections with traditional sources of wealth and power, but had a very highly developed sense of cultural obligation. The city was a network of learned societies, artists' associations and discussion groups. How could the house that Mackintosh built for the publishing family of Blackie be anything but a reflection of those distinctive circumstances? Hill House was the embodiment of a dream of a particular way life, of a certain view about the status of the Glasgow elite, whose roots were in Scotland, but who were also eager to establish their city as a metropolis with connections in the cosmopolitan new world of international culture.

Hill House overlooks the Clyde estuary, a short railway journey from the centre of Glasgow, with the shipyards that created the city's prosperity safely out of sight. With its circular, pointed turrets topped in grey slate, and its white rough-rendered walls, it is a house whose imagery derives from Scotland's collective memory of its past. But Mackintosh brought to this image his own highly individual sensibility. The facades of Hill House are graphic, composed of a flat, restless series of interlocking planes, undercut by a carefully proportioned grid, delineated layer upon layer. Mackintosh's client was a successful second-generation publisher, for whom this home was also a

workplace: the library in the house was as much a place to work as Blackie's office within the city, while the entertaining rooms were places to communicate the company's success and values. Indeed, it was Blackie's art director who recommended Mackintosh for the job in the first place.

For the Blackie family, with their seven servants, Mackintosh created a world of white walls and sunlight that, in the context of the soot-streaked, smoke-filled atmosphere of Glasgow, was a startling vision of another, quite different world. And that world permeated every corner of the house, from the spatial qualities of the public rooms and their relationship with one another, to the detail of each decorative aspect. The beds in the master room, the cupboards, the light fittings: they were all in a sense part of a single design. This was a house with a front and a back: there wasn't a servants' hall exactly, but there was a laundry, a coal cellar and a boot room, to say nothing of the scullery, the kitchen, the larder, the pantry and the wine cellar. On the ground floor was the library, the drawing room, the dining room, a morning room and a hall. At 744 square metres (8,000 square feet), Hill House would be large enough to accommodate at least six contemporary homes. Despite its white-and-purple interiors, it was full of open fires, a challenge to the longevity of the aesthetic that demanded high maintenance, which is to say adequate staff. The very fact of white walls could be seen as a reflection of the affluence of its owners. It would not be they who would be called on to clean every surface and thus maintain uncompromised its pristine state. It was a remarkably specific plan:

each room had a tightly defined purpose, tailored to that role. On the second floor of the house, the layout resembles a hotel more closely than an early-twentieth-century house. A special room, complete with a window, is dedicated to accommodating the linen. The master bedroom has its own dressing room (the lavatory and the bathroom do not open directly on to it, even though the plan clearly annexes them to the main bedroom).

The house is split in two, a division that is organized around a primary staircase used by the adult members of the Blackie family, and a back staircase that connects the service wing with the housemaids' rooms. This sensitivity to the social geography of the house was the starting point that shaped the direction of domestic architecture throughout the nineteenth and early twentieth centuries. Such houses are commonly described as single-family homes. But they were actually built to accommodate a household, and were designed to minimize social friction as much as possible for individuals of widely different status, all contained under the same roof, who would only be brought into contact with each other at clearly defined and signalled points.

In the early years of the century, the technical issues facing contemporary architecture were already well defined. But the results were far from the iconic houses of modernism that have burned their way into our subconscious. The house as the machine for living in was still some way off.

Hill House, outside Glasgow, was Charles Rennie Mackintosh's greatest domestic project. With its conical stair turrets and render and slate roofs, it recalls Scotland's historic houses, but its graphic facades were entirely new. Given the soot-streaked environment of Glasgow, the white walls of Hill House's main bedroom (top right) promised a new way of life.

Hill House

second floor

first floor

ground floor

10m

30ft

2

The birth of the modern movement
1910–1920

If modernity has its origins in the Enlightenment, the modern movement in architecture, with which it should not be confused, began to formulate around the time of the First World War. It was shaped by developments in painting such as purism – Le Corbusier's response to cubism – and influenced by cultural innovation in many different fields. Its roots were not just in Paris (where Le Corbusier settled), Weimar (where Walter Gropius opened the Bauhaus) and Vienna (the birthplace of architectural modernity): its abiding strength was that it drew on a multitude of sources beyond these centres.

Charles Rennie Mackintosh – as some critics have suggested – was more than a major architectural figure in his own right, but was also, at least in part, an inspiration for the Viennese explosion of creativity around the turn of the century. His work, built in Glasgow – at that time a city at the cutting-edge of both industrial and aesthetic creativity – attracted international attention. Hermann Muthesius published Mackintosh's designs for the *Glasgow Herald* newspaper offices, and so helped spread his reputation in the German-speaking world. Mackintosh won the competition for the hypothetical House for an Art Lover, turned into physical form only 90 years later, which was equally, even in the form of drawings, a significant factor in spreading knowledge of his work.

Mackintosh was clearly a strong influence on Josef Hoffmann in particular – who in 1903 actually made the pilgrimage to Glasgow – and the Viennese Secessionists in general. They picked up his predilection for chequerboard patterns and shared his view of a conjunction of architecture with the decorative arts. Mackintosh's own career was cut short by the circumstance of personality and temperament. He translated himself from an architect into a watercolourist of distinction when his professional relationships with his architectural partners broke down. At the point at which his architectural career petered out, his work was clearly making some sort of a transition from the Arts and Crafts roots of his early designs, and his improvisations on themes drawn from vernacular Scottish building intercut with modernism, that suffused his later work. His remodelling of a house in Northampton for the Basset Lowke family designed after he left Glasgow appears to suggest that he had embraced the fashionable motifs of art deco rather than the purism of Le Corbusier. As a result, it is hard to claim Mackintosh as an unambiguous modernist. Interestingly, Basset Lowke went on to commission Peter Behrens, who wasn't one either.

Antoni Gaudí was the focus of a similar outpouring of idiosyncratic creativity in Barcelona a little earlier in the twentieth century, without necessarily attracting overseas followers in the same way as Mackintosh. Gaudí was an inventor of genius, exploring radical uses of materials and aesthetics, which were at the same time rooted in a very particular cultural landscape. Well before the turn of the century, the Palau Güell, a grand house in the heart of Barcelona's most densely built-up quarter only a step away from the Ramblas, had demonstrated just what he was capable of. Simultaneously baroque, Moorish and Catalan in its references, it was spatially complex, and based on the constant search for new techniques and means of expression that was to characterize Gaudí's later work for his patron Güell, such as the Parc Güell, as well as projects for other clients such as the Casa Milá apartment block. Both Mackintosh and Gaudí were motivated in part by an ambition to reinforce a sense of national identity in two small, rapidly modernizing nations who were both associated with larger national groupings: Britain and Scotland, Spain and Catalonia. But the most powerful centre of architectural invention at the beginning of the twentieth century was Vienna. A city which, according to any view of architectural history that took the concept of the *Zeitgeist* with the slightest seriousness, ought to have been a decadent, spent force. This was the capital of an empire rapidly coming to the abrupt end so eloquently portrayed by Robert Musil in his great unfinished novel *A Man Without Qualities*. It was a view that was echoed by some of the most powerful Viennese critics of the period. Adolf Loos himself saw Vienna as a provincial, or primitive anachronism, marooned at the extreme end of civilized Europe, unable even to equip its soldiers with satisfactory boots. Many notable Austrian architects began leaving the country well before the First World War: Loos moved to Paris after a three-year spell in America. Rudolph Schindler, Richard Neutra and others emigrated to California. They found an America where Louis Sullivan, and subsequently Frank Lloyd Wright, were making their

Frank Lloyd Wright's
Robie house in Chicago
(1908–9) redefined the
way that space worked
in the domestic interior.

names. The great twentieth-century maverick and popularizer was always keen to seek an audience in the wider world beyond the narrow limits of architectural culture, and through the pages of the *Ladies' Home Journal*, he promoted his ideas of what the contemporary house could be, and tailored it, in theory at least, to a budget that was within the reach of the wider middle class. He was also to realize a remarkable series of houses in and around Chicago, from the Dana house to the Robie house, a family of designs that had their roots in the ideas of Sullivan, and a particular view of American culture, but which would shortly attract the attention of a generation of European architects, particularly after 1910 and 1911 when Wright's work was published in two volumes by the German publisher, Ernst Wasmuth. And while Wright was ready to give full expression to a new interpretation of space, and was certainly not shy of portraying himself as the single guiding force behind modern architecture, his work was rooted in a fundamentalist, elemental idea of what the house should be: an essentially romantic idea of a place that was at the intersection of hearth, soil and nature. While the European modernists at this time had eliminated the open fire as a primitive throw back, preferring electricity or gas as a modern, invisible, efficient means of heating, it was precisely this quality of primitivism that persuaded Wright to make the hearth the central focus of his homes, a paraphrase of the place of fire in the earliest human communities, a source of warmth, protection and conviviality.

Despite everything, for a brief, but very intense period, Vienna was the place that gave birth to architectural modernity, just as it was also discovering Freudian psychoanalysis, and pushing at the edges of the conventionally acceptable in art and music. Otto Wagner had already created an underground railway system for the city, which, while it might have chronologically lagged far behind London and even Budapest, was architecturally far more distinguished than any of its rivals. Vienna had demolished its city walls to create the Ringstrasse far later than most of its European peers had undertaken the task of modernizing themselves. And yet under Otto Wagner's leadership in the last decade of the nineteenth century and the first years of the twentieth century, the city had an unmatched wealth of architectural talent, and a commercial elite with the will to put it to work, despite the often bitter controversy that sometimes accompanied their efforts.

Of this group, it is the second generation of Adolf Loos and Josef Hoffmann who, with no love lost between them, grabbed most of the critical attention when the first definitive accounts of modernism were being written. But there was a much wider range of talent and opportunity in the city in the years after 1900 than that represented by these two poles.

Otto Wagner's career spanned the transition from traditional – what might perhaps more appropriately be called representational – architecture to modernity, and he emerges as one of the most complex figures of the period. It was Wagner who bolstered the career of his Slovene protégé, Jože Plečnik, while Hoffmann also emerged with a considerable debt

Antoni Gaudí built houses and apartments in Barcelona. The powerful, original vision apparent in the Casa Milá of 1906–10 went beyond conventional expressions of Art Nouveau. Gaudí's sculptural creativity was matched by his ingenious use of new materials, such as the ceramic fragments that decorate the Casa Milá's roof.

Casa Milá

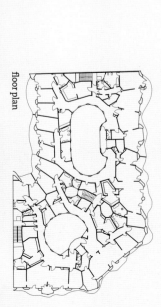

floor plan

Palais Stoclet

Completed between 1905 and 1910, the Palais Stoclet is the expression of a new kind of modern luxury, expressed by Josef Hoffmann's use of marble, both inside and out. Marble, framed by metal bands, gives the house the image of a large-scale piece of decorative art.

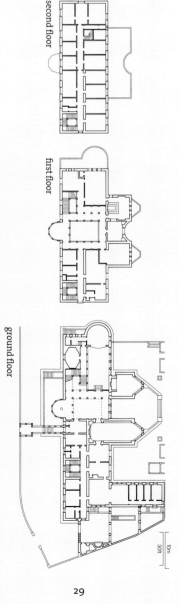

second floor

first floor

ground floor

10m

30m

Ludwig Wittgenstein's design for a house for his sister (top), completed in 1928, marked the end of Vienna's period as the world's centre for architectural innovation, one that began with Otto Wagner's own house of 20 years earlier (below).

to his teaching. Wagner moved from formal classicism to the remarkable achievement of the Post Office Savings Bank of 1904–12 with its use of aluminium as a decorative embellishment for its stone facades, its white stone, glass-roofed central hall and its specially designed furniture and light fittings.

In the field of individual housing, Wagner's strongest inventions were the two villas that he built for his own use on the edge of Vienna, one after another. The first was a Palladian pavilion of 1886–88. The second, designed in 1905, at the same time as the Post Office Savings Bank, and built between 1911 and 1912 on Bujatigasse (not far from his earlier house), was from a different world in its cubic purity. In sharp distinction to the propaganda of both left and right that modernity in architecture was a reflection of a progressive social programme, it is worth remembering that the Post Office Savings Bank was actually started as a reactionary response by Vienna's German nationalists to the cosmopolitan nature of Austro-Hungary's existing banking institutions.

Josef Hoffmann was later to adopt the role of an educator, taking on the leadership of Vienna's Hochschule für Angewandte Kunst, and of the Wiener Werkstätte, with its commercial application of a new approach to design and the craft traditions of the decorative arts – ranging from glass and silverware, to furniture. In Vienna, his architectural achievements included the austere but spatially supple design for the Purkersdorf sanatorium of 1903–7. But his greatest domestic work was in Brussels, where he built the Palais

Stoclet in the years leading up to the First World War. Hoffmann began work on the Stoclet house in 1905, and completed it five years later. This was a house that brought art, architecture and design together. Hoffmann was an architect as well as a brilliantly gifted designer of domestic objects and furniture. Influenced by Wagner, he designed the house as an exquisite object, delicately mixing white stone with metal inlay strips on its facades, subverting its apparently classical manner with an asymmetric facade. This was a house that could not have been conceived of at any earlier moment in history, and yet in which all the aesthetic and social elements were in fact the translation of an ancient concept of the house into a contemporary idiom.

The Palais Stoclet was built at a moment when new technologies were available, but only at a cost that put them out of reach of the mass market. It was the product of a brief cusp in time, when the technical issues of modernity were in place, but had not yet escaped into the wider world. The Stoclet family and their contemporaries had access to petrol-engined automobiles that were just about to be transformed by mass production, but hadn't been: production of the Model T Ford didn't begin until 1908. The Stoclet's class would have possessed a car, but hired a chauffeur to drive it, and would have accommodated them both in the 1910 version of a stable. The electric vacuum cleaner had also made its appearance. It too initially began as an artefact that was the preserve of household servants, rather than the householder. The Model T Ford was driven by its owners, just as the Electrolux appliances that followed

Mass production, demonstrated by Henry Ford's Model T of 1908, revolutionized not so much the construction of houses, as the ideology of the architects who designed them (top). Early domestic appliances, such as the Hoover vacuum cleaner (below), were initially aimed at servants rather than householders.

1. 'The Story of the Poor Rich Man' appears in English in L. Munz and G. Kunstler's *Adolf Loos, Pioneer of Modern Architecture*, 1966.

the earliest vacuum cleaners were operated not by servants, but by householders. The Palais Stoclet could accommodate a car without anything having appeared to have changed, either in the nature of the house, or of its urban setting. Mass production would very shortly transform everything, including the entire relationship of every house to the city, and of the car to the house. It is only the availability and wide dissemination of technology that gives power to trigger huge change: when innovation has become so widespread as to be invisible.

When architects realized what was going on in the new car factories, the building industry suddenly began to seem hopelessly outdated to them. Fordism could turn out high-performance affordable precision-engineered cars, while a construction site was still stuck in the Middle Ages or earlier, and the resulting houses looked the part too.

Adolf Loos mocked the architecture of this period, perhaps not Hoffmann directly, but certainly Henry Van de Velde. As he saw it, they were in danger of fading into overheated irrelevance. In his satirical essay, *The Story of a Poor Rich Man*, of 1900, Loos writes:

'Once it happened that he was celebrating his birthday. His wife and children had given him many presents. He liked their choice immensely, and enjoyed it all thoroughly. But soon the architect arrived to set things right, and to take all the decisions in difficult questions. The master greeted him with pleasure, for he had much on his mind. But the architect did not see the man's joy. He had discovered something quite different and grew

pale. "What kind of slippers are these you've got on?", he exclaimed painfully. The master of the house looked at his embroidered slippers, then he breathed in relief. This time he felt quite guiltless. The slippers had been made to the architect's original designs. So he answered in a superior way, "But Mr Architect, have you already forgotten? You yourself designed them". "Of course", thundered the architect, "but for the bedroom. They completely disrupt the mood here with these two impossible spots of colour. Can't you see that?"' [1]

Loos's own output was limited: a big commercial block at the back door of the Hoffburg Palace, a couple of houses in Vienna and another in Prague. But it had a highly suggestive echo in the house that the philosopher Ludwig Wittgenstein built in Vienna for his sister Margarete. Wittgenstein had trained as an engineer under the influence of his father, a steel magnate, and an important supporter of cultural innovation in Vienna. But his real talents were in other directions. He wrote his *Tractatus Logico-Philosophicus*, which established him as one of the key minds of the twentieth century but, traumatized by the impact of the First World War, he was in emotional turmoil in the 1920s and – partly in a therapeutic attempt to engage him with the everyday world – his sister involved him in the design of her substantial new house in one of Vienna's inner suburbs. Wittgenstein approached the task in a way that was quite different from the mainstream of architectural culture, at that, or indeed, any other time. It was an exercise in the application of pure reason and the intellect, that was

in one sense entirely outside time. For that reason, even today the house has a quality that seems entirely free of stylistic mannerisms, even in its late-twentieth-century incarnation as the Bulgarian Cultural Centre for Austria. And yet it does have in its mathematical purity a sense of the Vienna of a decade earlier than its actual creation between 1926 and 1928. If anything, it takes the rigour of Loos's earlier work to a logical conclusion. It is the architecture of fundamentalism.

This is a house in which it is clear that a mind of the highest order has been at work. Every proportion, every transition from one space to another, reflects the merciless application of intelligence. As the American artist Donald Judd was to remark half a century later, 'proportion is the act of reason made visible'. And nowhere is that more marked than in the Wittgenstein house. Each wall was pierced by openings whose relationships to each other, and to the walls in which they were situated, was considered down to the last millimetre, as were the implications involved in the act of piercing the wall itself.

3

1. Le Corbusier, *Vers une architecture*, 1923. English translation by F. Etchell, 1927.

The rhetoric of function
1920–1930

No one has done more to define the twentieth-century house than Le Corbusier. He provided not just the rhetorical underpinning that shaped the critical landscape for domestic architecture, but also much of the poetic invention that has characterized the development of the modern house. After moving to Paris in 1916 and establishing his own architectural practice, Le Corbusier was preoccupied with new definitions of housing. He produced the Domino prototype block in 1915, with its standardized structural reinforced concrete frame, and followed it with the Maison Citrohan in 1920. The latter, with its double-height living space and elevated sleeping platform, was to characterize much of Le Corbusier's domestic architecture, and has haunted the architectural imagination ever since.

This was the moment that Le Corbusier set out his vision of the role that mass production could play in defining the modern house:

'There exists a new spirit. Industry, overwhelming us like a flood which rolls on towards its destined ends, has furnished us with new tools, adapted to this new epoch animated by the new spirit. The problem of the house is a problem of the epoch. The equilibrium of society today depends upon it. Architecture has for its first duty, in this period of renewal, that of bringing about a revision of values, a revision of the constituent elements of the house. Mass production is based on analysis and experiment. Industry on the grand scale must occupy itself with building and establish the elements of the house on a mass-production basis. We must create the mass-production spirit, the spirit of living in mass-production houses. If we eliminate from our hearts and minds all dead concepts in regard to the house and look at the question from a critical and objective point of view, we shall arrive at the house machine, the mass-production house, healthy, and morally so too, and beautiful in the same way that working tools and instruments which accompany our existence are beautiful. Beautiful also with all the animation that the artist's sensibility can add to severe and pure functioning elements.'[1]

It was also Le Corbusier who produced the modernist critique of the city itself: the dream of the endless extrapolation of the city through the repetition of the suburban box, stretching out of every major city. He put forward high-density apartment buildings, raised up on stilts to leave the ground free, as the alternative. And yet Le Corbusier continued to explore the house: almost as a classical ideal, an object in a landscape, a poetic celebration of the machine age.

But before Le Corbusier translated his ambition into a house that measured up to its speculation about mass production, Gerrit Rietveld had built what was technically much less ambitious, but which was in many ways even more challenging. Truus Schröder-Schräder was the woman who was as much the creative force that triggered the building of what, 70 years later, is still one of the most radical houses of the twentieth century, as its ostensible architect. She was a proto-feminist, locked in a troubled marriage to an older man with whom she constantly disagreed over how best to bring up their three children. Rietveld was a designer and craftsman who provided the formal inspiration, who made the drawings and models on which the house was based, and who ran the building contract. But it was just as much her house as it was his.

Rietveld was married too – he had six children, but became emotionally as well as professionally involved with Schröder-Schräder. Their relationship was far more complex and intricate than the conventional architectural view of the interaction between client and designer would allow. As Schröder-Schräder demonstrated so powerfully, there are certain individuals who have been able to extract a creative response from the architect's imagination, and who are not content to play the role of the passive consumer in that process.

Rietveld was originally a furniture designer with an informal architectural education. He was associated with the De Stijl group – which was dominated aesthetically by the painter, Piet Mondrian, and theoretically by Theo Van Doesburg. Rietveld was the third member of the triumvirate on which the movement was built, and uniquely among such groups, he was able to put design right at the centre of its identity, rather than considering it, as was much more common, to be a peripheral interest.

The De Stijl manifesto was published in 1918 in the Netherlands, which, while remaining outside the conflagration of the war, was obviously deeply affected by the carnage all around it. 'The war is destroying the old world with all that it contains: the pre-eminence of the individual in every field', the manifesto claimed. The movement called on 'all those who believe in the reform of art and culture to

2. The De Stijl manifesto was published in issue 1 of *De Stijl*, October 1917. It is quoted in Reyner Banham's *Theory and Design in the First Machine Age*, London 1967.

Two symbols of the twentieth-century design revolution: Pierre Chareau and Bernard Bijovet's Maison de Verre, Paris (top) and Gerrit Rietveld's Red/Blue chair (below).

destroy those things which prevent further development, just as in the new plastic arts, by removing the restriction of natural forms, they have eliminated what stands in the way of the expression of pure art, the extreme consequence of every concept of art.'[2]

Mondrian, who was living in Paris, went home to the Netherlands after the outbreak of war, and had moved away from the cubism that dominated Paris in 1914, to become absorbed in abstraction. Subsequently, his art took space and its infinite, universal character as its principal subject matter. It was one of the strengths, and the novelties, of the De Stijl group – the neo-plasticists as they called themselves – that there was such an intimate connection between art, design and architecture.

Rietveld produced the first version of the truly astonishing piece of furniture that was eventually to become the Red/Blue chair as early as 1917. Originally it was monochrome – the colour came in 1923 – and it had the effect of translating the chair from an evocation of a piece of traditional Dutch vernacular design into something altogether different. It was clearly a translation of the spatial qualities of a De Stijl canvas into a physical object. Rietveld continued to explore this territory. Some of his experiments, such as his sideboard of 1919, had the quality of architecture in themselves. With its overhanging surfaces and its clearly expressed structural frame, the piece could be read as an evocation of a Frank Lloyd Wright Prairie house.

Rietveld was producing ostensibly utilitarian objects with just as much emotional intensity

and power as the supposedly quite different category of objects that are characterized as 'high art'. It was of course part of the rhetoric of a revolutionary cultural movement such as De Stijl to deliberately break down such supposedly artificial barriers. But it is enlightening to see the verdict of posterity on Rietveld's experiments through the unflinching indicator of financial value. An 'original' Rietveld chair sells at auction for a fraction of what an 'original' Mondrian canvas will command, though the meaning of 'original' is an ambiguous concept when applied to a chair designed in an era of mass production. Even more oddly, a chair that does carry the imprimatur of Rietveld's own hand, preferably as distressed and battered as possible, will be worth not only far more than a brand-new, and therefore presumably more serviceable edition of the same chair, but considerably more than one of the houses that Rietveld designed just three streets away from the Schröder-Schräder house a few years later.

Rietveld was recommended to the young Truus Schröder-Schräder as a designer who would be prepared to create a refuge from the conventional marriage that she clearly found so stifling. When her husband died, she turned to Rietveld to design a new house that would reflect a fresh start, a house that embodied her own approach to life, and offered a chance to bring up her young children in her own way. It was a house that was conceived specifically to allow for a close and intimate relationship between the children and their mother, rather than exiling them to a nursery. It was Rietveld's first major architectural work, marking the

start of a long career, but one that would never produce anything with quite the same force.

And there the house sits, in the unlikely, provincial setting of Utrecht, at the end of a dark-brown brick terrace of heavy dull houses that seem to exemplify everything that Truus Schröder-Schräder was running away from. It collides with, and yet manages to entirely ignore, its neighbours, orientating itself at 90 degrees to the terrace. Here is Schröder-Schräder deliberately turning her back on the city in which she had lived with her husband. The house once looked out over open country, and though it only has three elevations, it appears to be a free-floating object, lost in infinite space. The urban context of the house has changed radically: Utrecht has continued to grow so that the house is no longer on the edge of town. More damagingly, an elevated motorway has sliced through the city just a few feet away from the house's front door. Towards the end of her long and eventful life, Schröder-Schräder threatened to demolish the house, which by this stage she shared with Rietveld himself, and move to a more sympathetic environment if Utrecht went ahead with its threatened road building plans. In the event she decided to stay, but at considerable personal cost.

In some ways, the Schröder-Schräder house, perhaps more than any other house, has burrowed itself deep into the consciousness of the twentieth century, suggesting that the individual home can be the touchstone that defines architectural culture. This was not a conventional design beneath a radical surface in the manner of so many houses that adopted the

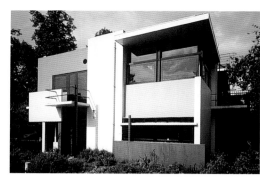

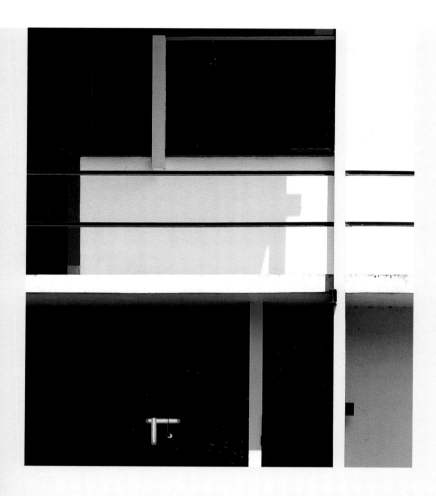

Schröder-Schräder house

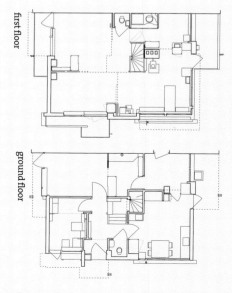

first floor

ground floor

Gerrit Rietveld's background as a cabinetmaker clearly informs the refined structure of the Schröder-Schräder house: the interior has few fixed walls and sliding screens are used instead. The most radical house of its day, it is tacked on to, but turns its back on, a conventional terrace of houses.

Villa Savoie

Le Corbusier's Villa Savoie in Poissy of 1929 is the embodiment of the modern house as a purist object, floating in an idealized landscape. The structure, carried on pilotis, displaced the traditional cellular layout of the house. The roof terrace of the Villa Savoie becomes an internal landscape.

roof

first floor

ground floor

Margarete Schütte-Lihotzky's Frankfurt kitchen of 1927 is the ancestor of every fitted kitchen in the world (top). Marianne Brandt's teapot of 1924 brought the Bauhaus into the parlour (below).

visual language of modernity, but which nonetheless clung to the familiar, even traditional aspects of affluent domesticity. The Palais Stoclet of Josef Hoffmann, for example, supported a way of life that would have been utterly familiar 200 years earlier. It presupposed wealth, servants and certain spatial arrangements.

The Schröder-Schräder house was anything but that kind of cosmetic treatment. Despite its setting on what was at the time the extreme edge of a comfortable Dutch city, it was a house that was designed to accommodate a very different way of life from that pursued by her neighbours. The most powerful first impression, despite its apparent spaciousness, is how small it actually is, with just two floors and a total of 139 square metres (1,500 square feet). The house, as much as anything, was an experiment in the way in which architecture could shape the relationship between a mother and her children, the youngest of which was aged no more than six when Schröder-Schräder moved in during 1924.

This was not a house which created barriers between the members of the household: rather it forced them to live in the closest proximity one with another. The living and dining areas are upstairs, along with all the bedrooms. Of these, only that of Truus had fixed walls; everything else was no more than a sliding partition without any acoustic insulating properties. The only escape for adults from the domestic life all around them was the library downstairs.

The house is the embodiment of the De Stijl aesthetic, in which one space melts into another. It feels as

if it is at the intersection point of endless planes that sketch in an idea of infinite space. This impression is underscored by the way in which the photographs that Rietveld himself approved were taken with all the windows swung into the fully open position, projecting at 90 degrees from their respective walls. The image is of a house that had no limits or cellular spaces, and which instead accentuated the indeterminacy of glass and solid, of wall and window plane, with terraces and balconies further disrupting the finite qualities of the external walls.

This image is reflected not just in the facades of the building, but also in the way in which one internal space interacts with another. The sliding timber partition offers no acoustic privacy whatsoever between Truus Schröder-Schräder's bedroom and the living and dining rooms. There is even less privacy between the two other sleeping spaces, in which the children grew up to maturity, forever aware of each creaking floorboard. The upper level could be transformed by sliding and folding back partitions to create one entirely open space. There is in this arrangement a reminder perhaps of Rietveld's origins as a cabinetmaker: the house was conceived as an ingenious mechanism, one that was not so far removed from the work of a master craftsman creating an intricate mechanism to be applied to a complex piece of furniture. Literally, this is a machine for living. Nor does it rely for its impact on the use of lavish materials: they are instead plain and humble. The house's power comes not from tactile qualities, or ostentation, but

Eileen Gray's own house, the E1027, was designed in 1926 at Roquebrune, Cap Martin. The house is approached from above, by a series of steps and paths leading down the terraced hillside (top). The design of the interior provides a unity between the architecture and the specially designed furniture (below).

3. Margarete Schütte-Lihotzky, quoted in an interview in Vienna by Tulga Beyerle, 1998.

from ideas about how life might be lived, for better or worse, in a radically new way.

Like Rietveld's furniture, most famously the Red/Blue chair, this is a design based on workmanlike qualities. It was revolutionary precisely because it was so accessible. For a moment, it was the Vatican of modernity, or perhaps the agitprop train of revolutionary design. Yet it is now a museum piece, scraped sadly clean of every trace of the patina of the lives of the remarkable people who once lived here. Parties of visitors are meekly herded into docile groups, protected from contamination by their disposable moon boots, which they slip on in an airlock at the entrance and are then led through the house by guides.

Rietveld and Schröder-Schräder's complex personal and professional relationship is a reminder of the problematic nature of the notion of the 'client'. The traditional architect's idea of a client is an abstraction, a bureaucratic cipher that negates any kind of personal interaction in the creation of a building. Against all the evidence to the contrary, it is a relationship that is conventionally represented as an insulating barrier that separates the architect from the world of ambitions and aspirations that actually shape buildings. It is a fantasy that has served to make a holy grail for the architect out of the brief, a concept that is specifically designed to keep the professional away from the reality of creating a house based on a complex mix of prejudice, dream, fantasy and budget, and offers instead a sanitized, rationalized abstraction. The client, according to this view, does nothing more than put forward the brief, while the architect

responds with the 'solution'. In reality, the client is most unlikely to produce a coherent set of functional requirements and then retire tactfully, leaving everything to the architect until it is time to pay the builder.

It is not for designing any single house that Margarete Schütte-Lihotzky will be remembered, but for the radical approach she brought to one particular aspect of the home, and of the way in which she developed a conception of a more generalized sense of responsibility for architects towards the anonymous occupants of social housing. Not clients as the concept was once understood – the government bureaucracy responsible for the brief and the budget for social housing – but the actual user of social housing was, for the first time, at the centre of an architect's vision.

The kitchen before the 1920s had not been the subject of much architectural attention: it was like the boiler room of a ship, another world, populated by crew, rather than passengers. As a result, the design of the kitchen was treated very much as the interior of a garage is today. With a very few exceptions, such as the monumental creations of Lutyens in the servants' hall, or the remarkable palm tree columns of the Prince Regent's kitchen in the Brighton Pavilion, it was pragmatic and utilitarian, rather than an aesthetic statement. But after the end of the First World War, the focus began to shift rapidly, for two main reasons. Firstly, the architectural profession became increasingly interested in social housing, in which there were no servants. Thus the kitchen became a principal element in the interior. The

imperatives of functional design in the kitchen answered the need of architects, who were searching for the raw material to put to a function that they could follow with form. The supposedly utilitarian processes of food preparation and cleaning were much more susceptible to the analysis of functionalism than the more fluid areas of the domestic environment such as the living room. Secondly, a gradual shift in middle-class life was underway which was eventually to put the kitchen rather than the living room at the centre of domestic life. This last phenomenon was in part the result of a gradual elimination of domestic servants, but also had something to do with changing preconceptions of the nature of domestic life. Either way, it is Margarete Schütte-Lihotzky who has a substantial claim to being recognized as a pioneer in both fields. In 1915, Schütte-Lihotzky had been one of the first women to study architecture in Vienna at the Academy of Applied Art, but while most of the school was enthusiastically pursuing the decorative style of Josef Hoffmann and the Secessionists, Schütte-Lihotzky was more interested in functionalism. As her student projects show, although she could draw beautifully and brought a refined elegance to her work, from the beginning she saw architecture as a social art. Even as a student, she worked on social housing projects. 'What attracted me to architecture was the very concrete task of serving the people', she has said.[3]

Behind the icing-sugar facades of the city, Vienna was going through a traumatic social upheaval marked by poverty and sickness. While Egon Schiele aestheticized tuberculosis, Schütte-Lihotzky actually caught the disease. With the encouragement of her professor, Oskar Strnad, she went out of her way to meet ordinary working people as a student. In the wake of the collapse of the Austro-Hungarian empire after the war, Vienna struggled to accommodate a flood of refugees from the east. Schütte-Lihotzky worked on schemes to cope with the burgeoning shanty towns around the edges of the city. She spent her evenings touring squatter shacks, a candle in one hand and her architectural drawings in the other, helping the refugees install running water and electricity for themselves.

But what really earned Margarete Schütte-Lihotzky a place in history was the Frankfurt kitchen. She had met Ernst May, the German architect who was building pioneering social housing in Frankfurt, and was invited to join his team. For five years in the 1920s, she produced a series of designs for standardized kitchens installed throughout Frankfurt's new flats. These have a strong claim to be seen as the ancestor of every fitted kitchen in the world.

Schütte-Lihotzky's designs for kitchens were elegant as well as economical. There were neat rows of storage bins and racks, and work surfaces designed to be easily cleaned. She devised a prefabricated concrete sink for one version of the kitchen, to keep costs down. Given the need to cram everything into the smallest possible space, washing was combined with cooking in some cases, and she designed bathtubs that came with a lid that provided an extra work surface when not in use.

Schütte-Lihotzky designed her kitchens to be practical. She used wide sliding doors to connect the kitchen with the living room, which allowed mothers to keep an eye on their children. She was equally practical about planning. She persuaded the City of Frankfurt to drop its scheme to accommodate single women in hostels. Under her influence they were allocated apartments integrated with conventional family housing. 'Rather than putting working women in a ghetto, it made more sense to house them with families [and] it allowed women who weren't working to earn a little extra money from washing or cleaning.' The kitchen was slowly being transformed from something like a workshop into something very much like a factory. In turn, this would serve as the starting point for a kitchen that, while it looked to be about work, was actually much more to do with the status of the owners.

Schütte-Lihotzky's kitchens were still places in which the effect of the consumer appliances industry had yet to make its mark. The oven, usually gas, but sometimes electric powered, was beginning to make its presence felt. But the refrigerator was still utterly exotic – restricted to America, and a rarity even there. Keeping food fresh was done by passive environmental controls such as the ventilated larder. What Schütte-Lihotzky also offered was a humane and practical alternative to the utopian notions of apartment blocks with communal kitchens, and communal eating facilities.

If Schütte-Lihotzky took on the kitchen, Le Corbusier provided the rhetorical basis for a sunlit bathroom at the heart of the house: 'Demand a bathroom looking south,

in one of the largest rooms in the house or the apartment: the old drawing room for instance. One wall to be entirely glazed, opening if possible on to a balcony for sun baths: the most up-to-date fittings with a shower bath and gymnastic appliances', he proclaimed, with the fervent zeal of a missionary zealot. The Villa Savoie bathroom wasn't exactly the ideal bathroom as Le Corbusier had proclaimed it, but it was, with its undulating floor and its built-in Roman tub, a radically different conception of the bath.

In *l'Architecture Vivant*, of 1927, Eileen Gray wrote her own description of the E1027 house, designed for Jean Badovici between 1926 and 1929, for a site in Roquebrune. It was a small isolated holiday house, named around Gray and Badovici's interlocked initials. It was a house that clearly referred to several of Le Corbusier's aesthetic principles, but it was transformed by the intensity with which every detail, fitting and piece of furniture was considered. 'Theory is not sufficient for life and does not answer to all of its requirements... [architecture] is not about constructing beautiful ensembles of lines, but above all else, about constructing habitations for man', she wrote. Nobody interpreted Le Corbusier's exhortations with more poetry in the detail than Gray, with her intricate mechanisms for storing clothes, with mirrors and lights set in them, hinged and folding.

Sadly, E1027 – along with the murals that Le Corbusier, who had built his own holiday cabin nearby, added uninvited to the pristine walls of the house – is derelict and graffitied today, despite wide recognition of its significance. Pierre Chareau and Eileen Gray both suffered from the excessive territoriality of the architectural profession: 'we are architects, you are decorators' was the subtext to much of the initial response towards them. They were self-taught, or taught outside the conventional architectural system, and yet both of them produced work that was impossible for the mainstream to ignore, and which was to go on resonating as an inspiration. It was Le Corbusier who coined the rhetorical formulation of the house as a machine for living, but it was Pierre Chareau who, in 1928–32, actually built it in the shape of the Maison de Verre, the apartment and surgery that he created for Doctor Dalsace, the wealthy Parisian gynaecologist with a practice on the Left Bank. This was not simply the rhetoric of functionalism: it was a remarkable, poetic synthesis of metal and glass. Nor was the Maison de Verre a piece of homespun hand-crafted timber like the Schröder-Schräder house: its aesthetic more resembled a handmade motor car such as a Bugatti. It is contained within a courtyard, crammed into the constraints of an eighteenth-century urban block and reached through a passageway from the street. The house signals its presence with a facade of glass brick that conceals more than it reveals: a glass curtain that allows the double-height living room inside to be suffused with light.

Chareau worked on the Maison de Verre with the Dutch architect Bernard Bijvoet, and together they produced a remarkably rich work that not only attracted Le Corbusier's passionate interest while under construction, but which was discovered in the 1950s by James Stirling and Richard Rogers, and

through them inspired a generation of so-called high-tech architects. They were enthralled by the spatial qualities of the house, with its complex layers of interlocking spaces, as well as the way in which the idea of mechanism was the aesthetic point of departure for much of the house: the wheels that opened the windows; the expressed service ducts; the switches, each celebrated with jewel-like precision. Chareau, who had a background as a decorator of de luxe interiors, used extraordinary, supposedly industrial materials, such as studded-rubber walls and perforated steel, to powerful effect. The specially designed furniture went beyond steel and iron however, as Chareau designed a relatively traditional sofa.

If it was the bentwood of Michael Thonet that had revolutionized the furniture industry in the nineteenth century, it was the experiments at the Bauhaus of Marcel Breuer and others with tubular-steel furniture that was to be the inspiration for a new approach towards furniture in the twentieth century. Breuer's furniture was to be regarded as one of the 'necessary instruments of contemporary life', rather than limited by the use of one material or another: 'Every day we are getting better, in the end, we will sit on resilient air columns', he said. And in 1926, Breuer produced a filmed version of how this might actually happen: a cantilevered seat holds the sitter in place, without actually touching, then the chair vanishes altogether, and the occupant is left levitating.

The Bauhaus, which emerged from the industry-orientated Deutsche Werkbund movement, was not, when it started, an

institution that included an architecture course. It had as its driving ambition the creation of an aesthetic philosophy capable of dealing with an integrated view of modern, industrial production. With the move in 1925–26 from Weimar to Dessau, Walter Gropius used the construction of a new Bauhaus building and associated housing for the school's masters as a test bed for new designs that could make the leap into commercially available products. It was some of these designs that were to provide the licensing income that kept the school afloat in the increasingly difficult climate of the 1930s. The school's exploration of furniture in particular set the pace. Breuer, who first came to the Bauhaus as a student, made the inductive leap to the cantilever chair after seeing an Adler bicycle on the streets of Dessau, with its tubular-steel frame – strong, yet lightweight – put elegantly to work to create handlebars. Why not use the same material for making a strong, simple and economical domestic chair? The result was the Wassily chair, named after Wassily Kandinsky, in whose house it was first used.

For Breuer, who was still in his early twenties, it was a remarkable achievement, and one that went far beyond a single design. In his tenure as head of the furniture workshop at the Bauhaus, he explored a whole repertoire of modular storage, tables and free-standing structural units that were to set the agenda for most furniture design, both domestic and commercial, for the rest of the century.

Tubular-steel furniture, especially in its most extreme form – the cantilever chair – was an

emblem of modernity: a crucial signifier, a test of taste. For many it represented the negation of all the qualities conventionally regarded as embodying domesticity. In the houses of Wassily Kandinsky and Lázló Moholy-Nagy, designed by Gropius and furnished by Breuer, this was precisely their purpose. But in terms of genuine machine-age techniques, the use of tubular steel was no more advanced than the laborious hand construction used to give the white boxes of international style houses the appearance of mass-made mechanized production. Bending a steel tube into a neat radiused curve is a skill well within the capability of the most basic gas fitter's workshop.

The birth of the tubular-steel cantilever chair was accompanied by considerable controversy and a flurry of lawsuits over its precise authorship. The left wing Dutch architect Mart Stam met Breuer before the unveiling of what came to be known as the Cesca chair, and produced a cantilever chair of his own in prototype form, fabricated from gas pipe with standardized angle-fitting connections. Mies van der Rohe also designed a series of cantilevered chairs – the Brno used flat steel – of which there was also a swooping tubular-steel version.

The lawsuits came and went. By the 1960s, the original designs were being copied around the world, though not with the names of the original designers attached to them. And by the 1970s, the original rhetoric had come true: tubular-steel furniture had become not only universally available, but cheap.

The end of the romance of the machine

In 1917, Marcel Duchamp installed a urinal and a hat rack in an art gallery and claimed that it was a ready-made work of art. Shortly afterwards, Le Corbusier installed a bidet in the bedroom of one of his houses.

Mass-produced objects, which had previously been treated as if they were invisible, were for once made visible. Duchamp was challenging conventional ideas about art. Le Corbusier was confronting his clients with the realities of hygiene, one of the fundamentals of everyday life that, while produced in enormous quantities, had always been conventionally concealed from public view. Designers and architects looked for ways to construct a culture that made sense of a new relationship between a machine-orientated, mass-market economy – one in which the standardized rather than the particular were said to have the greater significance – and which had still to come to terms with the impact of serial reproduction on the meaning of art.

Le Corbusier had had a personal experience of this clash between craft and industrial production in the most telling way. His father's workshop, producing hand-crafted watch faces, had been bankrupted in 1918, at least in Jeanneret senior's own mind, by the impact of mechanization. It was, however, an essential part of the ideology of the modernists to embrace mechanization. It was Mies van der Rohe who wrote in an article published in the third issue of the radical magazine *G*, in 1924:

'I see in industrialization the central problem of building in our time. If we succeed in carrying out this industrialization, the social, economic, technical and also artistic problems will readily be solved. It is not so much a question of rationalizing existing working methods as of fundamentally remoulding the whole building trade. Our technology must and will succeed in inventing a building material that can be manufactured technologically, and utilized industrially. This will lead to the total destruction of the building trade in the form in which it has existed up until now, but whoever regrets that the house of the future can no longer be constructed by building craftsmen should bear in mind that the motor car is no longer built by the wheelwright.'

Czechoslovakia at the start of the 1930s was a state that had only briefly been in existence since emerging from the wreckage of the Austro-Hungarian empire. With its German-speaking minorities increasingly being drawn into the orbit of Hitler's Reich, it was ready to unravel again despite transient prosperity. But for a period between the two wars, Czechoslovakia was a state that was proud to see itself as self-consciously modern. It had an arms industry as advanced as any in Europe.

The Tatra cars engineered by Hans Ledwinka formed the basis for much of the thinking that led to the development of the Volkswagen by Ferdinand Porsche. The Bata shoe factories were a model of industrial innovation, and brought with them the construction of a series of company towns that housed the Bata workforce in exemplary functionalist dwellings across Czechoslovakia. After the declaration of the Czech Republic in 1919, the Czech kings were reburied in Prague Cathedral, not in some nostalgic evocation of past styles, but on an uncompromising black granite catafalque. By any standards this was one of the most sophisticated corners of Europe.

Brno, in the south of the country, is just two hours' drive from Vienna. It has a baroque heart and a spreading ring of suburbs where prosperous villas enjoy distant views of the city centre. This is the context for the Tugendhat villa, perhaps the most well known of the domestic designs Mies van der Rohe completed before he moved to America. It was designed at the same time as the Barcelona pavilion, and Lilly Reich, Mies's long-term collaborator, worked on both projects. Despite their fame from the moment that they were completed, both projects turned into ghosts. The Barcelona pavilion was demolished as soon as the 1929 Exposition was over, to be reconstructed only in the 1980s. And the house in Brno vanished from view behind the Iron Curtain after 1948.

When Grete Weiss Low-Beer married Fritz Tugendhat in 1927, her parents gave the couple enough land to build their own house as a wedding present. With such a high-profile site in a city that had already put itself at the forefront of architectural innovation, the Tugendhats opted for a house designed by an architect that would reflect their aspirations. This was not just a wedding present, and not just a house; it was always going to be a cultural statement. After briefly considering a Czech architect for the project, the Tugendhats hired Mies van der Rohe, perhaps the most celebrated architect they could have contemplated, to do the job. Mies, by that time a considerable figure in European architecture – having just completed the master plan for the Weissenhof Siedlung in Stuttgart – was a towering presence in the context of Brno.

The Tugendhat house is based on a steel-frame structure, expressed in the famous cruciform nickel-plated steel columns that were Mies's trademark. It is planned on three levels that step down a precipitous slope. From the street frontage, the house looks as if it could be a bungalow, with just a single-storey entrance wing facing the street. Below this, the rest of the house is orientated entirely towards the garden, with windows on just one elevation. At street level, it opens up to incorporate a terrace and housekeeper's lodge.

The house took the technological ambitions of modernity very seriously. Technically, it was ingenious. It had central heating, of course, but there are also much more ambitious features, such as push-button, electrically operated retractable windows and a photoelectric cell which, in the evening, would automatically close the door between the terrace on the entrance level, and the street. There was even an extract fan in the kitchen. The television wasn't available yet, but the family would have gathered around a wireless set to hear news of the darkening political landscape of Europe.

The early photographs of the house show two of Mies's cantilevered Brno chairs, designed specifically for Tugendhat, facing one another across a table. They tackled the millennia-old task of supporting the human posterior at a comfortable level off the floor with the same mechanistic precision

that an aeronautical engineer would bring to the profile of an aircraft wing.

Lilly Reich's hand can be seen in the sensuous planning of the main living room, the choice of materials, and in particular, its colour scheme with its acid-green leather upholstery. The completion photographs show a teddy bear poignantly sitting on the exotically figured wooden furniture in one of the children's bedrooms.

The choice of Mies van der Rohe as architect attracted some local criticism, portrayed by some as a snub to local talent. As a German, he would certainly have raised the question of the Czechs' ambiguous feelings towards their neighbours. German was still the language of the Bohemian elite in Czechoslovakia, while Hitler was soon to use the German-speaking minorities within the country as the pretext to dismember the new Republic in 1938.

When the house was completed in 1930, there was considerable scepticism about its livability: criticism which Grete and Fritz Tugendhat were quick to counter. After an onslaught on the house led by the leftist critic Karel Teige, they wrote to the architectural magazine *Die Form* to make it clear that despite all the speculation to the contrary, they actually liked their house, although: 'It is true one cannot hang pictures in the main room, and one cannot break the stylistic uniformity of the furniture by introducing a new piece into a room – but does that mean our personal life is being suffocated?'

The Tugendhats moved to Venezuela just ahead of the invasion of Czechoslovakia by the Nazis. They escaped, abandoning most of their

Designed in 1928, Ludwig Mies van der Rohe's Tugendhat house, built on a hillside overlooking Brno, reflects the spatial richness of its contemporary, the Barcelona pavilion. This was the villa for which Mies designed the Brno chair, and devised his trademark nickel-plated cruciform steel column.

upper floor

ground floor

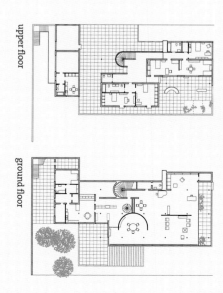

Frank Lloyd Wright was almost 70 when he built Fallingwater in Bear Run, Pennsylvania, for Edgar J. Kaufmann, in 1936. It was a weekend house that arose as part of the landscape, combining daring cantilevered terraces with living rock and rough field stone. Fallingwater demonstrates Wright's attachment to the idea of the hearth as the atavistic centre of the home.

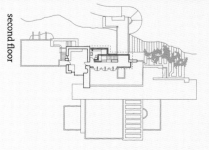
second floor

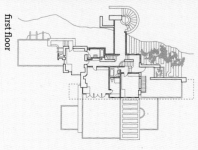
first floor

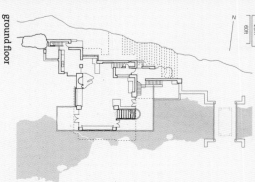
ground floor

Fallingwater

Alvar Aalto designed the Villa Mairea in Noormarkku, western Finland, for Maire Gullichsen in 1937–38. Together, they established the Artek company in order to manufacture Aalto's furniture designs, such as the laminated birch moulded plywood stackable stool (below).

furniture and even their books and personal papers. In their absence, the house was badly damaged, requisitioned by a range of invaders, crudely restored, and then restored again. The Gestapo are said to have taken over the house for a while, then came the Messerschmidt aviation bureau. When the course of war shifted the front line, the Germans were displaced by a Red Army cavalry unit which bivouacked in the house complete with their horses – a fate that seems to have overtaken more than one domestic icon of the modern movement: though in the case of Le Corbusier, it was German, not Soviet horses that did the damage. When Czechoslovakia was subsequently swallowed up by Stalin in 1948, the Tugendhat house was left stranded outside the mainstream of Western cultural life as little more than a memory. Few Western critics got to see it, and it was lucky to survive without being demolished. Even though it had been lived in for less than a decade, it was already one of the key pieces of architectural innovation, a design that had shaped the evolution of the architecture of the twentieth century. And yet for almost 50 years, there was nothing but a set of photographs to remind the world of just how significant a house this had once been. The Tugendhat house is now re-emerging once more in a totally changed political reality, having played its own part in the fall-out from the last acts of the Cold War: it was used as the setting for the final negotiations in the divorce between the Czechs and the Slovaks in 1990.

Built in 1936 by Frank Lloyd Wright, Fallingwater at Bear Run, Pennsylvania, was a weekend house for the Pittsburgh department store millionaire Edgar J. Kaufmann. For its architect, already almost aged 70, it was a triumphant comeback after a decade in the professional wilderness, and considerable financial hardship. Fallingwater, perched on the edge of a waterfall, its interiors invaded at various points by outcrops of living rock, has captured the popular imagination like no other piece of twentieth-century domestic architecture. Wright was to become the most lionized architect of the century in America, celebrated with a postage stamp, and even a song from Simon and Garfunkel, composed when Paul Simon was himself briefly an architecture student.

The house is sensational with its melodramatic tiers of gravity-defying cantilevered terraces jutting ever further out over the waterfall and flashily playing off smooth-poured concrete with rough field stone. It is a tour de force of Americana, like a Cadillac designed by Harley Earl.

Curzio Malaparte – born Kurt Erich Suckert, of a German father and an Italian mother – was one of this century's more idiosyncratic literary figures, who was responsible for an equally remarkable house, one that demonstrated long after it was built that there were far more strands to contemporary architectural culture than the original authors of the myths of architectural modernism would ever have allowed for. Malaparte was involved with just one architectural project, his own house, built on the edge of a cliff top on the island of Capri. But it was a project that had resonances far beyond the conventional architectural world, and demonstrated that architecture is

an aspect of culture which is not just locked in a hermetic, professional world, but is shaped by a much wider constituency. Malaparte was a member of Mussolini's Fascist Party, even though he was imprisoned by them twice. He became a member of the Communist Party before he died in 1957, after a career as a journalist, cultural critic, playwright and author, and was also responsible for the Casa Malaparte on Capri, one of the most dramatic houses of the twentieth century. The extent of his involvement in the design of the house was in doubt for many years. Malaparte had originally engaged the Italian rationalist architect Adalberto Libera, who was responsible, among many other projects, for some of the key landmarks of Mussolini's expansion of Rome at EUR, the Expo killed off by the outbreak of the Second World War. Malaparte asked Libera to design a house for him, but never let go of its creative direction, and eventually took charge himself. This was not a house rooted in functional pragmatism. The Casa Malaparte was conceived as a literary work, a three-dimensional visual poem that is structured as a series of intense emotional experiences: some are evocative and rooted in memory, others are tactile, while still others are surrealistic juxtapositions, such as a big Tyrolean stove next to a classically inspired hall, or a glass window held in a precise frame and punched through a massive wall to reveal the tortured, twisted pillars of rock that emerge out of the sea far below the house.

It appears from the planning documents that Malaparte had already dispensed with Libera's services even before construction started, and that the final form of the house was the result of the input of many individuals including Malaparte himself, his builder, and a range of his friends. Work on the design of the house began in 1938: a number of schemes evolved, and Libera was to deny responsibility for the form of the house as it was eventually built.

From this complex and difficult process an extraordinary landmark emerged. With its famous stepped roof, the Casa Malaparte evokes a classical Greek theatre – like the ruins that survive just down the coast on the Italian mainland – and yet also incorporates sculptural curved concrete that clearly refers to the fashionable motifs of the 1930s. This was a house designed for a very particular existence: for a self-consciously anti-bourgeois individual, a man with no interest in conventional family life, a sensualist who was looking to make himself a place in which he could retreat to a setting for solitary writing and contemplation.

The house sits in a landscape so exceptional that, even as early as the 1920s, it was already the subject of a concerted official attempt to protect it from unsympathetic new development. Malaparte used his political connections to secure the necessary approvals. In a passage from his book, *La Pelle*, the writer relates in a fantastical episode how, on the eve of the battle of El Alamein, he played host to Field Marshall Rommel. The soldier asked him whether the house was already built when he bought it, or whether he built it himself. According to Malaparte, 'I replied – and it was not true – that I had bought the house as it stood. And pointing with a sweeping gesture to the sheer cliff of Matromania... and the remote golden glimmer of the Paestum shores, I said:"I designed the scenery."'

The Villa Mairea, Alvar Aalto's great domestic work, was designed for Maire Gullichsen, born Ahlström. The Ahlström family was one of Finland's great industrial dynasties. They still control a multinational corporation, originally based on paper and forestry, at the end of the twentieth century. Harry Gullichsen married Maire Ahlström, the granddaughter of the founder, in the 1930s. The couple met Alvar Aalto in 1935, through an introduction from Nils Gustav Hahl, an art critic friend of Aalto's. Together they established Artek, the company that has done so much to shape the identity of contemporary Finnish life with a distinct product-range of furniture, the best of it designed by Aalto himself. Aalto was also invited to work on the master planning of the Ahlström company towns. But it was the Villa Mairea, designed over a protracted period and finally completed just before the Second World War, that was the most distinguished achievement of the collaboration between architect and patron. The villa is at Noormarkku, in western Finland – well away from Helsinki – and is located on a compound of houses built by generations of Ahlströms from 1877. This is a house that is designed not just as a family home, but as a setting for a commercial elite anxious to exercise a cultural role in a deliberate attempt to influence Finland's view of itself, and its place in the world.

Maire Gullichsen had trained as a painter, and the house was in part conceived as a place to accommodate a distinguished collection of contemporary painting from around the world, but it was also a place in which to entertain visiting artists and writers, and in which to run a high-powered literary and artistic salon in one of Europe's remoter corners. The house's social rooms took on a major significance: the greatest of them is a sprawling 232 square-metre (2,500 square-foot) gallery. Just as important was the relationship with its forested setting that Aalto carefully made the starting point of his L-shaped plan. The Gullichsen house is rural not urban in its inspiration: beautifully crafted, subtle, complex and rich in its imagery. Completed just before the start of the Second World War, it stands as the last in the series of great modern houses of the pre-war generation.

Casa Malaparte

roof

first floor

entrance floor

10m
30m

A tense relationship between the writer, Curzio Malaparte, and the architect, Adalberto Libera, produced the dramatic Casa Malaparte on Capri, completed just before the Second World War.

Malaparte had no interest in conventional family life. Rather than a place for family breakfasts, the aim of the house was to frame a remarkable series of views, and to provide a sculptural roof.

5

In the 1940s, the advertising industry went to work to sell the idea of a new way of life to the masses. This example from the *Saturday Evening Post* was as much about the charms of mechanized appliances as it was about family life.

Untouched by the physical devastation of the Second World War, America experienced a period of unprecedented prosperity in the 1940s. It was a prosperity that created a new car-borne, suburban way of life, characterized by the building of the first edge-of-town drive-in shopping malls and the development of tract housing spread evenly across previously rural landscapes. And through its rapidly strengthening grip on the image-making capacities of the international film industry, this new and specifically American way of life served as a showcase for an avalanche of materialism that captured the imagination of the rest of the world. Entirely new categories of consumer appliances showered out of American factories – from the television set and the electric hairdryer to the first microwave oven, designed in 1947 by Percy le Baron Spencer. In themselves these were humble, even banal objects, but spun together into a dizzying whole, they created a powerful dream of domestic affluence, one that collided head-on with the austere architectural vision of modernism.

Three of the iconic houses of this period – Philip Johnson's own house (the Glass House) in New Canaan, Connecticut, built in 1949; Ludwig Mies van der Rohe's Farnsworth house in Plano, Illinois, designed and built between 1946 and 1951; and Charles and Ray Eames's house in Santa Monica, California, of 1945–49 – are superficially similar and all of them rely on exposed steel and glass walls. Indeed, both Philip Johnson and Charles Eames acknowledged their debts to Mies. But they responded to the impact of consumerism on the architectural

interior in very different ways. Mies suppressed objects as far as possible, banishing them at least from view and, if possible, omitting them altogether from the Farnsworth house. Indeed, the only place that the present owner has found to put family photographs is in the bathroom. With the exception of the sanitary fittings, Mies designed everything in this interior, furniture as well as architecture. There is no room even for art: what could compete with the sight of the meadow outside? Johnson, on the other hand, has no antipathy to things; indeed he celebrates them and of course flatters his own taste at the same time by the careful choice of just a few items, which are turned into the objects of connoiseurship by their isolation. In the Eames house, however, the impact of domestic objects is controlled by the energy with which the two designers filled it with their own possessions, both precious and mundane, exotic and familiar, and even more, by their sheer abundance. The whole house is like an exquisitely ordered shop window, full of things, yet arranged in such a way that there is an apparent sense of control and discipline to them. In the Eames house, there are platoons of objects marshalled on the coffee tables, on shelves, hanging from the ceiling and attached to the walls, as well as things sitting on the floor and positioned on the beds.

Could Philip Johnson's Glass House ever have been built if Mies van der Rohe had never existed? Clearly not. Johnson was once Mies's leading propagandist. The young Johnson strutted around Germany in the 1920s and 1930s, getting much closer to Nazism than mere flirting-

Once he had moved to the United States in 1937, Walter Gropius resumed both teaching and architectural practice, putting his belief in mechanization to the test with his designs for prefabricated housing. He is seen here with Konrad Wachsmann, pioneer of industrialized buildings, supervising the assemblage of a packaged house.

1. Philip Johnson in conversation with Janet Abrams in 'From Matt Black to Memphis and Back Again', *Blueprint* magazine, 1989.

range, living the good life fuelled by his inheritance at the time of the great inflation and investing a tiny slice of it in a Cord in which to ferry the impressionable Mies around Berlin as if he were a character from *Cabaret*.

Johnson, along with Henry-Russell Hitchcock, established Mies's American reputation with the 1931 international style exhibition at the Museum of Modern Art (MoMA) in New York. When Johnson eventually decided to step back from the role of cultural and political dilettante and actually train as a professional architect, he chose to study with Walter Gropius in the gilded surroundings of Harvard, rather than in the more utilitarian setting of Chicago's Illinois Institute of Technology, where Mies himself eventually landed a teaching job just in time to save himself not so much from persecution by the Nazis, but from the historically much more damaging fate of remaining in Germany for too long. It was a decision that Mies, acutely aware of his own relatively humble social origins as the son of a stonemason, when set beside those of the conspicuously officer class of Gropius, did not fail to notice.

In the 1950s, it was Johnson who effected the introduction to Phyllis Lambert that secured Mies the crucial commission to build the Seagram building in Manhattan for her father, and in return Johnson was invited to design the Four Seasons restaurant at its base. Subsequently, Mies and Johnson fell out, as Johnson mischievously tells it, after nothing more historically significant than a whisky-fuelled late-night argument about the merits or otherwise of the Dutch architect Hendrik Berlage.

Before that, Johnson had built the Glass House in New Canaan: the physical incarnation of his graduation project at Harvard, submitted to Walter Gropius and Marcel Breuer, but of course in reality aimed at Mies. He completed it two years before Mies finished his own landmark domestic design in America, the Farnsworth house at Plano, a weekend retreat outside Chicago for a wealthy doctor, Edith Farnsworth.

Johnson designed his home in 1949, when he was completely familiar with Mies's plans for the Farnsworth house (which had already been exhibited at MoMA). Long after, Johnson told the British critic Janet Abrams: 'Mies called my house a rather bad copy of his. He never liked it. I was never trying to do the same things as him, though I was certainly vastly influenced by his work.'[1]

Contemporary architectural historians now eagerly attempt to find vividly sexual meanings in both these projects, a measure perhaps of the way that the subject of architecture has come to reflect wider intellectual fashions. Johnson's Glass House, almost always photographed in isolation from the rest of the accretion of buildings that gradually populated the estate, is now routinely – and positively – described in terms of the architect's homosexuality as 'transgressive', 'exhibitionistic' and 'camp'. Contemporary feminist readings of the Farnsworth house compete with the constantly recapitulated interpretation of the relationship between Le Corbusier and Eileen Gray in their efforts to present it as the architectural equivalent of the Ted Hughes and Sylvia Plath catastrophe.

The very idea of a glass house,

Charles and Ray Eames produced a single piece of great architecture: their own home in Santa Monica, California, but their furniture was to prove even more influential. Their storage units, partitions and timber chairs blurred the distinction between the domestic world and the office. The aluminium chair (top) was both a technical and aesthetic tour de force.

one which has become so much a part of the contemporary landscape of modernism as to be taken for granted, runs directly counter to all the most atavistic views of the home as a place of shelter and security. Two decades before either Johnson or Mies had built their houses, Walter Benjamin had remarked that 'to live in a glass house is a revolutionary virtue'. Revolutionary the Farnsworth house certainly was. Internal walls all stop short of the exterior; the bathrooms are accommodated in a single internal block; and only a built-in cupboard separates the sleeping area from the main space. The whole house is on a single level, hoisted up above the flood plain of the nearby river and appearing not to touch the ground – a visual gesture of both practical and symbolic significance. Edith Farnsworth maintained that the intellectual ruthlessness of the house was foisted on her against her wishes by the architect. She refused to pay the final bill to the contractor, claiming that Mies had recklessly exceeded her budget, and she professed shock that he expected a fee for his work as an architect. As Alice T. Freidman's book *Women and the Making of the Modern House* suggests, Farnsworth had given him medical advice without expecting payment, so why should Mies expect to get paid for rendering her a professional service? More to the point, she went public with her dispute. In the pages of an issue of *House Beautiful* magazine of 1953, she portrayed Mies as a sinister Teutonic totalitarian, imposing his authoritarian aesthetic approach on an innocent America. Mies went to court over his unpaid fees and eventually won the case. Farnsworth had known Mies for some years and

had been an enthusiastic participant in the exhibition of the design for the house in 1947 at MoMA. Yet she claimed the finished house was not what she had been promised and that the experience of actually living there was too oppressive. The wall-to-wall glass undeniably produced a strong sense of psychological pressure, especially at night. The fact that Mies designed a second bathroom in the house's central core specifically so that lunch guests would be spared the sight of Farnsworth's dressing gown hanging on the back of the door is presented by unsympathetic critics as implying voyeuristic exploitation. *House Beautiful* quotes Dr Farnsworth as saying:

'The truth is that in this house with its four walls of glass, I feel like I am a prowling animal, always on the alert. I am always restless. I don't keep a garbage can under my sink. Do you know why? Because you can see the whole "kitchen" from the road on the way in here, and the can would spoil the appearance of the whole house. So I hide it in the closet farther down from the sink. Mies talks about "free space" but his space is very fixed. I can't even put a clothes hanger in my house without considering how it affects everything from the outside. Any arrangement of furniture becomes a major problem because the house is transparent like an X-ray.'

But despite this outburst, Farnsworth chose to live in the house for 20 years. And the image of the X-ray is not one that is always presented as having negative connotations. Le Corbusier once used the image sympathetically when he suggested that 'the house is a body X-rayed by the sun. Its girders are a skeleton of steel, its ramps and

In October 1949 Raymond Loewy – a first-generation American industrial designer – made the cover of *Time* magazine, together with a range of his designs, from the Coldspot refrigerator to the Greyhound bus. Loewy, who defined good design as 'an upward sales curve', contributed to the creation of the myth of the all-powerful designer.

sloping floors serve as muscles... [and] plumbing and ventilation ducts are its veins and bowels.' The house was eventually acquired by Peter Palumbo, the well-known collector of twentieth-century houses – he also bought the Maisons Jaoul – who treats it as one of his most treasured possessions.

The other message of the Farnsworth house was its demonstration of the way in which America had eclipsed Europe as the creative centre for modernism, while transforming its meaning. The Farnsworth house was the physical translation of Mies's thinking about design in an American context.

Between them, Mies, Johnson and Charles and Ray Eames gave the architecture of the steel and glass house a new, and perhaps specifically American character. This character seemed to reflect an acceptance of the landscape in a way that was not possible in the urban context of Europe, and perhaps also – in the case of the Eames house at least – an innocent, optimistic embrace of the potential of American industry and the abundance that it could now support. The other clear difference was the fireplace. While Mies never believed in them, Johnson made the fireplace the central focus of his house, slicing it out of a free-standing brick cylinder that also accommodated his bathroom. In so doing, Johnson deferred to the all-American precedent established by Frank Lloyd Wright that the fireplace was the heart not just of the traditional, but also of the contemporary home.

Charles and Ray Eames built themselves a house and studio in Santa Monica, California, that in its own way was to have as much

of an impact on the architectural imagination as Rietveld's Schröder-Schräder house. Interestingly, both Eames and Rietveld designed significant pieces of furniture that reflected their own architectural philosophy. Both houses are lightweight, have a distinctive spatial freedom and use colour in strongly graphic ways. And both Rietveld and Eames were to some extent from outside the architectural mainstream. But Rietveld's house belongs to a steam-age, propeller-driven era, while the Eames house is – despite the debt that Charles Eames acknowledged to Mies van der Rohe – more than anything a celebration of America's coming of age as a nation of industrial plenty. Built as one of a series of Case Study houses, with the encouragement of the publisher John Entenza, who promoted the houses through his California-based magazine *Arts and Architecture*, the house is based on the intelligent, adaptive use of industrial components, materials and techniques originally developed for quite different purposes that offered powerful possibilities in other areas. As Reyner Banham pointed out, the house may have used off-the-shelf components, but Charles and Ray Eames didn't have just any shelf to choose from. Theirs was a shelf stacked high with the products of the world's most sophisticated industrial system, and the spare poetics of the house were the result of the superior quality of American industrial production. This is not a ready-made in the provocative sense of a Marcel Duchamp urinal: it is a careful, considered aestheticization of the ready-made. Nor was the Eames house and the whole California movement an isolated

phenomenon. Gropius himself, working with Konrad Wachsmann, was designing prefabricated industrialized houses at this period.

The Eames house itself was modest in scale and democratic in intent. Plenty, in the Californian context, did not mean ostentation or servants. It implied an intimate relationship with the landscape, and a simple form that allowed for spatial complexity. Clearly, the house is dependent on a vastly different mindset from the craftsmanship of William Morris, although in many ways it is just as anti-urban as that which Morris was proposing a century earlier. And like Morris, it brought into being a whole school of followers – although Morris would have been unlikely to sympathize with the English high-tech architects who found the Eames house an abiding inspiration for their work, delighting in the matter of factness of its construction and the sense of competence that the Eameses brought with them. The Eames's extraordinary experiments with aluminium castings for furniture have managed to retain a sense of immediacy and freshness, while the technology that produced the components that the Eames house was built of now belong to history. Think about a typical car of the late 1940s that represented the leading edge of technology on the day that the Eameses moved into their house: the Eames house still looks part of the present, but the cars of its youth now look absurdly antediluvian in comparison. The Eames's aluminium group furniture, or the earlier steel rod and ply chair of 1945, however, are still made the way that they where when they were first introduced, and they still have just as much formal power.

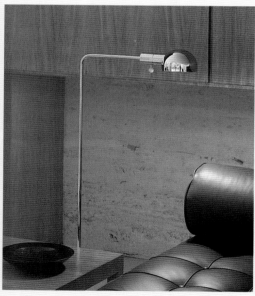

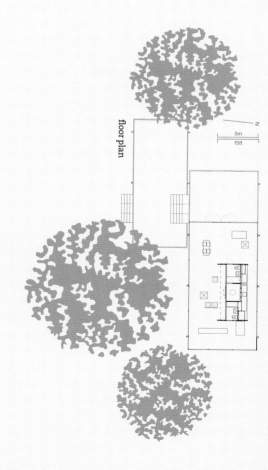

floorplan

5m
15ft

At the Farnsworth house in Plano, Illinois, all sense of enclosure vanishes, and Mies van der Rohe's house appears to float in free space. A turbulent relationship between Mies and Dr Farnsworth led to bitter recriminations and a lawsuit. Farnsworth spoke of a sense of oppression caused by Mies's glass walls, although she continued to live in the house for 20 years.

Glass House

Philip Johnson built his Glass House in New Canaan, Connecticut, before the Farnsworth house was complete, but he knew the plans well and acknowledged his debt to Mies. Johnson's house is rooted firmly on its site with its dark brick floor recalling the earth. By contrast, the Farnsworth house floats above the ground.

floor plan

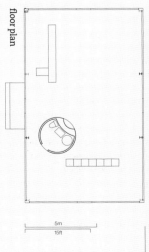

5m
15ft

N

63

Built as part of a series
of experimental Case
Study houses in
California after the
Second World War, the
Eames house depended
on a careful selection of
prefabricated industrial
components that were
transformed by the
designers' sensibility.
The double-height
interior is characterized
by the frank expression
of its steel frame, as
well as the Eames's
remarkable collection
of found objects.

Eames house

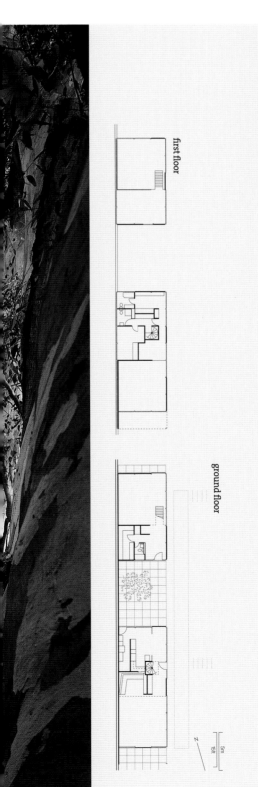

first floor

ground floor

15ft

5m

6

Furniture from Gordon Russell, such as David Booth's sideboard of 1951, helped set the style for the Festival of Britain (top), but real leadership came from such designs as Arne Jacobsen's three-legged Ant chair of 1952 (below).

In the 1950s, Britain emerged from the war into a period of austerity that was in many ways even bleaker than the deprivations of the Blitz. British Design at that time was a cottage industry, run by enthusiasts, or else slightly raffish gents – the Wells Coates and the Hugh Cassons – who treated the subject as a sideline to their principal activities as architects. And the work that they produced – posters promoting BOAC's new propeller-driven Argonaut airliners, white enamel Ascot gas heaters, or labels for TCP antiseptic bottles by British Alkaloid, were well meaning, if derivative of what others were doing in America or Scandinavia.

Set beside the new Alfa Romeo by Pininfarina, Olivetti's latest typewriter by Marcello Nizzoli, or Gio Ponti's flamboyant espresso machine, this was feeble stuff indeed. Even the Festival of Britain – a product of the 1940s, though it was not actually staged until 1951 – was not, at least to some contemporary eyes, the triumph that it is now depicted to have been. The architect James Stirling for example, remembered going to London's South Bank to see the exhibition, and coming away with a sense of disgust. Disgust at what he saw as the missed opportunities and the sentimental compromises of the design that he found there. And yet, if British design was hardly at the cutting edge in that period, Britain was the country that managed, almost single handedly, to create the modern profession of design. Designers discharged from war work, many of them in the Ministry of Information, felt a real sense of purpose as they set about the task of post-war reconstruction. Design was considered to be a utopian affair.

It was the means through which the nation reassured itself that a future was possible. Its economy in ruins, Britain had no chance of manufacturing the consumer goods that the modern world appeared to promise. But design in the post-war years could be used to give the appearance, if not the substance, of plenty.

In his role as President of the Board of Trade, Sir Stafford Cripps established the Design Council – or the Council of Industrial Design, as it used to be called. This was the same Stafford Cripps who went on to become Chancellor of the Exchequer in the Attlee government of 1945, and was responsible for a regime so unrelievedly grim that Evelyn Waugh was moved to describe his tenure as 'years in which the country appeared to be under enemy occupation'. Yet Cripps and Hugh Dalton, his predecessor as Chancellor and at the Board of Trade, were champions of design as an instrument of government policy for just the same reasons that Mrs Thatcher was, 40 years later.

Even before the war, as Dalton and Cripps acknowledged, everything from Czech glass to American fashion was so superior to their British equivalents that there was nothing that the government could do to stop them capturing the British market when the war ended. But one thing that did distinguish the 1940s' view of design from the attitudes of the 1980s was the high moral tone taken by its partisans. Design, to the pipe-smoking, bow-tied Reithians who made up the design panel of the Board of Trade, who ran the Council of Industrial Design, and who were to go on to stage the Festival of Britain, was nothing if it was not a

1. Stafford Cripps, BBC
Radio Archives, London.

Harry Bertoia's diamond
pattern lounge chair
of 1953 (top) was an early
post-war example of
a sculptor's approach
to design. Gio Ponti's
Superleggera chair of 1957
(below) is technically and
visually exceptional.

moral crusade. It was not, despite the alibi of industrial regeneration, primarily an economic issue. It was seen as a cultural question. Fake 'Jacobethan' wardrobes, electric lamps that looked like wax candles and coal-effect electric fires were all regarded as in some sense immoral. To look like something that you were not was a particular sin. In the days before affluence, there was a patrician disdain for vulgar materialism. Good design was presented as if it was about more than selling goods. But as Stafford Cripps revealed to the BBC, it was actually defined in terms of taste, and society's values:

'At home, our common objective is a standard of living. And we must not think of that desirable aim merely in quantifiable terms, regardless of its character, that is regardless of the quality our income can buy. You can have squalor and ugliness, even among riches. Neither the maker, nor the user can get real satisfaction out of ugliness or shoddiness. And a standard of living which fails to give pleasure and satisfaction is a fraud.'[1]

The idea that design is a moral issue is of course not a new one. In Britain, from William Morris onward, a certain strand of thought equated simplicity with virtue, and superfluous ornament with gross moral turpitude. At the turn of the century, the idea was exported from Britain to Vienna and Berlin, and in the 1930s, a wave of refugees from mainland Europe brought this same message back from the Bauhaus, cross-pollinated and amplified by the enthusiasm of Walter Gropius for a machine-age aesthetic. But design remained a minority interest. It flourished in London's Hampstead and in the weekend cottages of

Suffolk, a self-contained world, stocked with orange-spined Penguin paperbacks and studio pottery, but hardly anywhere else. It was a taste characterized by simplicity and restraint. Before the war there were just a few design-conscious firms, notably Jack Pritchard's Isokon, which had appointed Walter Gropius as its design controller and manufactured pieces by Marcel Breuer briefly in London before moving across the Atlantic. Anglepoise produced its famous lamp and the Chicago-based manufacturer Ekco made radios.

But in the 1940s, Britain's wartime emergency propelled the partisans of Morris and Gropius – previously the representatives of no more than a narrow elite – into positions in which they had access to the levers of power. Typical of this group was Gordon Russell, before the war a designer and manufacturer making furniture in the Cotswolds that attempted to blend the Englishness of the Arts and Crafts movement with a hint of rational modernism, liberally sweetened for British tastes.

Russell led the most remarkable attempt to impose the taste of the design elite on the masses that Britain has ever known in the form of the Utility Furniture Project. With nothing to spare for the domestic market but the few scraps of timber that the military didn't need, the Ministry of Supply restricted the production of domestic furniture to a list of just 20 approved items. Prices were centrally controlled and manufacturing anything but the Board of Trade-approved Utility Designs was punishable by a prison sentence. Right up to the 1950s, furniture was only available to the victims of bombing and the newly

The Maisons Jaoul in Neuilly-sur-Seine of 1954–56. The two linked houses designed by Le Corbusier reveal a profound aesthetic contrast to his pre-war purism, as represented by the Villa Savoie.

married. Their ration coupons bought them a strictly limited range of tables, chairs, wardrobes, beds and sofas that look tame enough to present-day eyes, but were greeted with stunned incomprehension and even derision by a furniture industry used to manufacturing reproduction Chippendale by the yard. Previous attempts at tampering with British tastes – a continual preoccupation of the proselytizers for modernism – had concentrated on exhortation and education. The masses would now be forced to buy good design, because nothing else was available.

The very idea that a government minister should be in a position to approve what the nation would be able to put in its living rooms seems inconceivable today. But at the height of a wartime command economy, such paternalism seemed entirely natural, and it spilled easily into the building of the post-war welfare state.

Utility furniture was presented as an important success, one that persuaded the national government's Labour members and the design pundits of the period that it might provide a model for the post-war reconstruction already being planned. But it is equally possible that the memories of war-time deprivation and compulsory good taste left Britain with a permanent anathema to the simplified modernity that seemed to have been an essential part of the war effort.

Gordon Russell played a leading role in establishing Britain's Council of Industrial Design in 1944 and went on to become its chairman. The council's approach had two strands. It set out to persuade the masses that design was a good thing. And it tried to badger industrialists into making better products. The great unanswered question was how to define 'better'. This was a period in which the British state intervened as never before in an attempt to determine in the most detailed form the shape of the contemporary house. Post-war reconstruction and slum clearance were treated as the highest priorities. Government architects worked on a range of prefabricated house designs, partly in an attempt to deal with the demand for housing from returning soldiers and their families after four years of bombing, and partly to provide an alternative for factories no longer needed for the war effort.

The Conservative administration of the 1950s had set up the Parker-Morris Commission with a brief to explore the optimum layout of the contemporary home, and codify its findings as the basis for the provision of all social housing in Britain. It prescribed the relationship between one room and another and delineated the size of the critical areas of the house. It specified the appropriate level of storage provision, as well as the likely size of the average household and provided standardized house plans that were used throughout the country.

Architects worked for the local authorities to design housing that was as good as they could make it. Most private developers built for profit. It was a period in which social housing, subsidized by the public sector, began to offer more civilized and generous space standards than the commercially available, private-sector equivalent. This was clearly an unsustainable and anomalous situation. To attract customers, private developers had to differentiate their products, in external imagery at least, from public housing. If architectural high culture was closely associated with public sector housing, the private house builders took the low ground. Technically and aesthetically inferior though they might be, the effect of the market was paradoxically to make them look more valuable.

As the world emerged from the austerity years of post-war reconstruction, it was increasingly obvious that the domination of architectural culture by Europe had come to an end. At the same time, the critical interpretation of architectural modernity in the terms that had been defined by Nikolaus Pevsner and his followers and bounded by Le Corbusier, the Bauhaus, the international style and their heirs, looked increasingly unconvincing.

America, Sweden and Latin America, unscarred by the war, were setting the pace in the design of the house as much as anything. And after the first flush of post-war reconstruction, they were joined by Italy and Japan, two states that began to establish their new identities in terms of design and architecture. In Italy, these were the so-called miracle years in which the northern half of the country at least finally made the leap from a virtually pre-industrial economy to position itself among the leading European industrial powers.

Since the days of Peter Behrens and the AEG, industrial design had moved a long way. The task of designers now was to tame industrial machinery and give it a character appropriate to the domestic context. Designers, aimed to domesticate machinery, explored

new colours, materials and unfamiliar visual languages. It was the Italians who took the lead in the process. Achille Castiglioni had designed the sculptural Phonola radio in 1940, and in 1948 Marcello Nizzoli designed the Lexicon 80 typewriter for Olivetti. Milan was able to employ the traditional craft skills of its old workshop-based economy – the leather workers, metalworkers and carpenters – creating the world's leading contemporary furniture industry. Old craft techniques could equally well be put to work on radical new designs. And workshop skills could be used to make the tooling on which advanced production techniques depended.

The 1964 Olympics in Tokyo, as defined by Kenzo Tange's stadium, marked Japan's establishment as a country that had not only rebuilt itself after the devastation of two nuclear bombs, but which had also made it clear that it was no longer content to imitate Western originals. It had, in architecture, as in many other areas of culture, established itself as a source of original ideas. Architecture has always been a significant means of expressing the establishment of the cultural ascendancy of one nation over another. Or else, of the centre over the periphery, and the expression of one set of values against another. Thus the European colonization of North and South America, Australia, India and Africa was quick to use architectural expression as a means of making explicit the relationship of power between colonizer and colonized. But also important was the relationship between colonist and imperial power, an ambiguous relationship in which there was both the need to create a sense of

Oscar Niemeyer's own house, overlooking Rio de Janeiro, helped to establish a Latin American architectural identity during the 1950s – in particular the use of reinforced concrete in the development of complex curved surfaces.

2. See James Stirling on the Maisons Jaoul in the *Architectural Review*, March, 1956, pp 154-161.

familiarity and legitimization, as well as an implied sense of loss, exclusion and inferiority. In Sydney and Melbourne, nineteenth-century British settlers built cities perched on the edge of a gigantic and largely empty land, and did their best to establish neighbourhoods that turned their backs on their context and recreated the suburbs that they left behind.

From the arrival of the Portuguese and the Spanish in the New World at the end of the fifteenth century, it was the architecture of the religious orders that accompanied the first soldiers and priests that permanently marked the hegemony of the Europeans. And for the next 400 years it was Europe that remained the inspiration, the point of reference, and of authority, through the language of architectural expression as much as through anything else. The baroque of the Portuguese in Latin America, just as much as the Palladianism of New England, and then subsequently the modernism of Le Corbusier in Brazil, were all marks of deference to a far-off metropolitan culture. It was only in the second half of the twentieth century that the former colonial states began to create their own sense of architectural identity.

While it is too much to say that it was architectural expression which created a sense of self-determination in these states, it is clear that national self-esteem coincided in many countries with the moment when a convincingly distinctive architectural language emerged, from Frank Lloyd Wright in the United States, to Kenzo Tange in post-war Japan. In Mexico, Luis Barragán occupied a similar position. Barragán managed to

encompass both tradition and modernity in a way that seemed to be particularly appropriate to the emerging identity of Mexico as a complex modern state. But each of these figures worked within the particular circumstances of a national context. Barragán's work was almost exclusively domestic: it was the product of the intense sun of Mexico, the blank walls of the ruins of the conquistadores, as well as the powerful geometry of pre-Colombian culture. But Barragán had also been to Europe, where he had seen that Le Corbusier's work was informed primarily by this kind of sensuous modernity. The powerful colour that infused all Barragán's designs was the very particular product of his Mexico, and its blazing, sun-filled skies. The quality of his spaces was infinitely carefully considered, each wall and window positioned with endless thought, the result very often of several attempts at building, altered after last-minute on-site inspections by the architect.

In Brazil, Oscar Niemeyer built himself a mountain-top house overlooking Rio de Janeiro's beaches in the early 1950s which puts a free-flowing plan on top of a remarkable site into a composition that is both sculpture and architecture. Like Barragán in Mexico, Niemeyer was helping to define a state's sense of itself.

This was also the moment when a revisionist view of what had already happened in the century took hold, and encouraged the development of a fresh synthesis of design. Just as Kenzo Tange, Luis Barragán and Oscar Niemeyer emerged as talents in their own right – rather than as dim peripheral

echoes of a distant European original – so the work of diverse groups from the early decades of the century, such as the futurists, the expressionists and the rationalists, came to be reassessed, not as blind alleys in the development of twentieth-century architecture, serving as temporary distractions from the main course of architectural evolution, but as major episodes in their own right. This critical reassessment could be seen as providing the permission for the exploration of a much wider range of possibilities for a new generation of architects.

At the same time, Le Corbusier, the most inventive of the pioneers, set out to redefine himself, much as Picasso continued to reinvent his art at the same period. This was the moment when Le Corbusier made a transition from the precision and purity of his mechanically inspired earlier designs to the rougher-hewn forms of his architecture in the 1950s and 1960s. The Unité d'Habitation in Marseilles realized at least in part his recurring vision for communal living. The exigencies of post-war France meant that the building used rough board-marked concrete, rather than the steel and glass that the architect had originally envisaged. The Maisons Jaoul, completed between 1954–56 in Neuilly-sur-Seine, took the theme of hand-marked concrete and rough brickwork as an end in itself – to the concern of some of Le Corbusier's admirers. It became not a machine for living, but a piece of three-dimensional sculpture of a high order. James Stirling, perhaps the most accomplished British architect of the second half of the twentieth century, found this project of particular significance to his own career.[2]

Habitat and IKEA were
to have an international
impact on the look of the
domestic interior.

The Maisons Jaoul signalled the transformation of Le Corbusier's domestic work from modern movement precision – the individual house cast in the image of a precisely delineated machine-made mass-produced object – into a much rawer expression that came to characterize his later work, evidenced by the rough concrete, gritty brick and articulated vaults of the Maisons Jaoul. It was only during a brief period in the late 1920s and early 1930s – when he worked with his cousin, Pierre Jeanneret, and more particularly with Charlotte Perriand – that Le Corbusier turned his attention to furniture design. In the 1950s and 1960s, he recycled the *objets types* that he had defined so many years earlier.

During this period, the range of widely available consumer goods exploded in numbers, as well as choice and variety. Logie Baird had invented the television set before the war. Its first commercial use in America was launched at the pre-war World's Fair in New York. But it was only in the 1950s that television's relentless onslaught on domestic life really got under way, and Henry Dreyfuss's television set for RCA in 1946 finally defined the modern form of the television as an object. The Ampex 600 portable tape recorder, manufactured from 1954 onward, created another new area of consumer durable, one that, like many others, has gone from rarity to universality and to obsolescence in the course of the last 30 years.

From 1951, Braun, the German consumer electronics company, recast its visual identity in terms defined by the Hochschule für Gestaltung in Ulm, the post-war successor to the Bauhaus, and applied it to radios, record players,

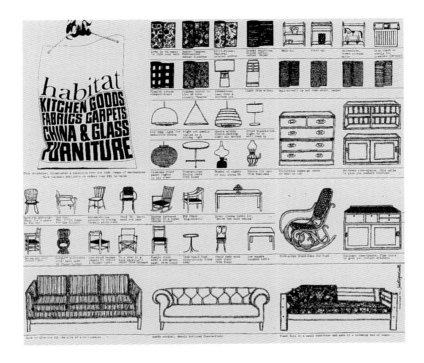

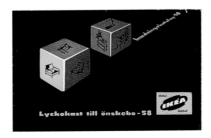

electric razors and to the company's new electric food processor in 1957. This was a brave attempt by a manufacturer to present its products as a reflection of a moral and cultural view of the world rather than as a short-term commercial expediency. Dieter Rams, the company's design director for 30 years, once described the ideal domestic artefact as being like a good English butler, 'invisible when not required, but ready to perform effortlessly well as soon as called for'. The artist Richard Hamilton was moved enough by the idealism of the Braun experiment to make its toasters the subject of his painting '$he' of 1958–61.

A wider gap began to open up between the American and the European idea of industrial design, such as that between Hoover's US-produced vacuum cleaner, designed by Henry Dreyfuss in 1954, and the REM vacuum cleaner that Achille Castiglioni produced in 1957. In America, size was of primary importance, while Europeans were more interested in the sculptural and tactile qualities of design.

Equally important was the change in the way in which consumers related to their homes. A new generation of retailers and decorating magazines attempted to make sense of this growing abundance for newly affluent consumers. The launch of Terence Conran's Habitat store and mail-order catalogue in London at the start of the 1960s attracted most of the attention in the English-speaking world at the time. Habitat supposedly contributed more to the popularization of modernity in domestic design than was ever achieved by the Design Council.

With a series of domestic designs in and around Mexico City, Luis Barragán synthesized a sense of Mexican identity, in particular through his use of colour and natural materials combined with the austerity of the European modern movement. Barragán's staircase transforms the house into a piece of sculpture.

Barragán house

7

The age of extremes
1960–1970

During the course of the 1960s, the architect, previously represented as a hero figure engaged in the construction of nothing less than a new Jerusalem, was precipitously demoted to the much more humble position of chief scapegoat for all the perceived ills of housing policy, and a misplaced reliance on novel construction technology. It was a dizzyingly rapid fall. At the beginning of the decade, Western countries reached a high water mark of prosperity and affluence that invaded every corner of the domestic world. And at the same time, nothing seemed beyond the reach of professionals and scientists. Hunger could be eliminated in the developing countries and, if only the intelligence of the architect and the planner could be brought to bear on the problem, the slums of the cities of the developed world could be abolished.

In America's suburbs, every house began to acquire a swimming pool, a boat parked on a trailer in the driveway, three-car garages and a barbecue pit. It was a dream that could still be presented in the advertising of the period without a trace of irony. The world fell head over heels in love with shiny plastic and chrome, with transistor radios and Mini cars. The possibilities of shape-making based on injection-moulded plastic techniques and inflatables helped to define the look of the period and glossy fibreglass invaded the living room. The texture of the interior was transformed as mouldings and elaborate architectural details were removed to provide seamless sheer surfaces and radiused corners.

Even though some of the definitive domestic objects of the period – Verner Panton's one-piece moulded plastic chair, the chrome-and-marble of the Arco light, designed by the Castiglioni brothers and Gaetano Pesce's inflatable Up chair – were never produced in large numbers, their impact was powerful nonetheless, reproduced constantly through the growth of popular magazines on decoration, in advertising imagery and in film. Such objects as the Up chair and the shapeless bean bag chair (from Zanotta, the Italian furniture manufacturer) represented an unparalleled degree of experimentation in the domestic interior. The objects that defined a consumer society were themselves being used to challenge the notion of consumerism. A chair with no fixed shape that sits without legs on the floor, and has no apparent reliance on the conspicuous qualities of craftsmanship, is deliberately flouting all the conventional signals of status.

Before technology came to be associated with Napalm, defoliants, pollution and conspicuous consumption, the future looked like something to be anticipated with optimism. And architecture was the profession that was leading us towards it. But by the end of the 1960s, the professional position of the architect was in a critical state. Its prestige had all but evaporated. The utopian visions born of the dreams of the early modernists and their realization in such works as Le Corbusier's Unité d'Habitation in Marseilles had been diluted almost beyond the point of recognition. They had eventually spawned the federally funded housing projects of the United States, and council housing in Britain. Despite the bold hopes that had accompanied their creation, these projects often turned out to be deeply flawed, both technically and socially: their demolition by dynamite began within 20 years of their construction. The failure of these projects, often for reasons far beyond the control of the architect, undermined the authority of the entire idea of modern architecture. It could be argued that by rushing to accept the blame for all that had gone wrong, rather than sharing responsibility with the contractors, politicians, housing managers and all the other infinitely complex cast of individuals that play a part in the making of public housing policy, the architectural profession was in fact just as much engaged in self-aggrandizement as it was in self-abasement. As far as the interior was concerned, the first flush of enthusiasm for plastic gave way to a regression into nostalgia for art deco or the rustic charm of Laura Ashley.

If public housing followed blindly in Le Corbusier's footsteps, then the individual houses of the period owed Mies van der Rohe even more of a debt. The austere glass box had become the model for the expensive weekend house, from Gordon Bunshaft's own home in the Hamptons onward, and these quickly lost their appeal: simplified forms and the very idea of building individual private houses began to be looked on with suspicion. Machine imagery was seen as anathema. Architects began to explore self-building and the counter-culture.

The fundamental optimism that had underpinned architectural modernity into the 1960s evaporated. The consensus view about what architecture should be was blown apart in the wake of what was a particularly troubled

time for authority figures everywhere, not least for those professionals who presumed to take decisions on behalf of the public. For two generations, the unchallenged view held that there was just one responsible approach to the design of contemporary domestic architecture: it had, it was alleged, history on its side, and the best interests of the masses at heart. It had its roots in functionalism and the international style. Suddenly that view was no longer tenable, and the discovery of this uncomfortable truth could be seen as having triggered a collective professional nervous breakdown. As America's great society blundered into the bloody swamp of Vietnam and its own cities began burning in a period of unprecedented civil unrest, the professions who had claimed to offer the country's cities a future were exposed as being bankrupt of ideas. There was, for a while, nothing to put in the place of the old certainties, and architecture marked time.

This intellectual vacuum made room for a range of once marginal figures: Buckminster Fuller's Geodesic domes were the model for a range of counter-cultural settlements in the California and Arizona deserts, though rather than use tubular steel, more often they made do with steel panels cut from abandoned cars. Paolo Soleri, once a follower of Frank Lloyd Wright at Taliesin West, created Arcosanti, his homespun utopia, in the Arizona desert. And work by such architects as Bruce Gough – who until this point were seen as outsiders producing little more than kitsch – was taken seriously.

But this hiatus did not last long. A new generation of architects in America, including Robert Venturi,

Michael Graves and Robert A.M. Stern, began to experiment with the design of single-family houses in order to explore a way out of the blind alley in which they found themselves. They wanted to be liked, and they set out to find a more crowd-pleasing architectural language. And to that end, they set out to destroy their intellectual father figures mainly through the means of a withering hail of sarcasm. Mies van der Rohe was the principal target. 'Less', according to Venturi was certainly not 'more', as Mies would have had it, but a 'bore'. Freed of the restraints of sobriety that had accompanied modern architecture, Venturi roamed the boulevards of Las Vegas, looking to learn lessons from popular culture to apply to high architecture.

The Vanna Venturi house in Philadelphia, that he designed for his mother in 1964, served as a kind of manifesto, albeit one of a very discreet and well-mannered kind, for his brand of allusive, complex architecture. Venturi was playing a game of double bluff. It was a house that was deliberately designed not to look as if it belonged to, or had been designed by, an architect. Look at its elevation and you could almost assume that this was a developer's tract house. Its gabled facades act as an obvious signal of domesticity. But on the inside, the layout reveals not a pattern-book plan, but one deriving from an architect who has devoted considerable scholarly effort to an understanding of the complexities and subtleties of mannerism. It could be seen as having it both ways. But for Venturi, the point was that the self-conscious avant garde had nothing to offer the real needs of clients. Architecture, in

Achille and Pier
Giacomo Castiglioni's
Arco lamp, designed
in 1962 (top); the world's
first all-transistor
portable television by
Sony, of 1959 (below).

his view, had a duty to make itself understood.

Le Corbusier, despite the problematic legacy of the Unité d'Habitation – which continued to remain as a glowering presence looming over public housing worldwide – and the ruthlessness of his approach to town planning, got off lightly by comparison with Mies. Michael Graves's painterly drawing technique is a deliberate echo, or an uncomfortable paraphrase, of Le Corbusier. His early domestic projects paid tribute to the master, though in a more colourful form, in such projects as the Hanselmann house in Fort Wayne, Indiana, of 1967.

As Graves attracted large-scale commissions, his domestic work took on an increasingly formulaic aspect, relying on the architect's translation of the language of classicism into a personal style, distinguished by an instantly recognizable palette of colours and an evocation of the turn-of-the-century opulence belonging to the Secessionists in his designs for furniture and tableware.

Richard Meier, once associated with the intellectual circles that nurtured Michael Graves and Robert A.M. Stern, spent most of his later career engaged on an apparently endless series of variations on the basic themes of Le Corbusier's visual language. Like Graves, Meier had produced a personal signature, which, as his success grew, was precisely what attracted his new clients to him. He made houses that recognizably carried his signature.

For Richard Meier, and for Peter Eisenman, the way out of the impasse of the 1970s was to return to the roots of the pioneering period of architecture from the 1920s, and to create an architecture of complete abstraction, shorn of any functional alibi. In Meier's hands it became a formula for the all-white architecture that became synonymous with corporate, as well as personal success. His Smith house, in Darien, Connecticut, completed in 1967, coarsens and inflates Le Corbusier, pumping up the original motifs on steroids. Instead of refined windows within white walls, he used huge glass planes, two and three storeys high, set directly into the walls, with the whole floating over a green lawn. Eisenman retained a sense of edgy avant gardism, refusing, for example, to refer to the houses that he designed at this period by their clients' names, but giving them numbers, as if they were works of art.

Britain managed to avoid the extreme tensions of American society. There, the most powerful piece of domestic architecture of the period was the product of a partnership between Richard Rogers and Norman Foster, and reflects a range of different but mostly optimistic meanings. Richard Rogers's career went through a curious watershed in 1998. Just at the point that a team of abseilers was busy putting the finishing touches to the skin of the Rogers-designed Millennium Dome in London, the Department of Culture, Media and Sport listed Creak Vean, the first house Rogers had a hand in building, giving it the same status as a Georgian manor house, or a medieval church. What was once cutting-edge design had passed into the comfortable sepia-tinted world of history in little more than 30 years. It is now hard to imagine just how radical Creak Vean had seemed in the context of when it was completed.

For an architect who has never had any time for nostalgia, it was a decision that cannot have failed to

provoke mixed feelings. Of course, it was a genuine recognition of a considerable achievement. But from now on, in the unlikely event that Rogers is called in to remodel Creak Vean's interiors, or to add an extension, he would first have to ask the permission of the art historians at English Heritage. Even replacing the vintage 1966 white enamel bath with something a bit more up-to-date could attract their censure: 'But Lord Rogers, how can you convince us that what you are planning to do is in keeping with Richard Rogers's design of 30 years ago, that distinguished architect whose work we have a statutory duty to protect?' And what are they going to do about the already updated shower fittings – insist that they are removed in the interests of period authenticity?

Perhaps this kind of thing is the inevitable outcome of the way that Britain's heritage lobby has spent the last 20 years playing grandmother's footsteps with a succession of ever-less sympathetic decades. First it was Victoriana, then it was art deco, and finally it was the 1960s. Each in turn went from being regarded as the decade that taste forgot, then became an acquired taste for amused insiders, before becoming a popular enthusiasm. Turn your back for an instant, and you find that the threshold dividing hopeless eyesores from priceless pieces of national heritage has crept another five years closer to the present.

But Creak Vean was exactly the kind of house, radical in its use of materials, unfamiliar in its shape, that architects like Rogers had to fight hard to get the chance to build at all, even though its sensitive planning and imaginative design is a rebuke to most contemporary suburban housing. If it hadn't been for Creak Vean, the course of British architecture over the last quarter of the twentieth century would have been very different. It gave a kick-start to the careers of Britain's two best-known living architects, as not just Rogers, but also Norman Foster worked on Creak Vean. It was their first job after meeting at Yale as post-graduate students.

Rogers's father-in-law, on the edge of retirement, wanted to build a country house – a place to go sailing, to accommodate boisterous family holidays and entertain friends. On the strength of the commission, Rogers and Foster came home to Britain and set up Team 4, an architectural practice that only lasted three years before Rogers and Foster went their own ways, but in that brief period it managed to explore most of the key strands in the thinking of 1960s British architectural modernism. There was nothing quite like Creak Vean anywhere in Britain when it was finished in 1966. The house is a tour de force that exploits to the full a magnificent coastal site perched on the edge of a narrow creek. It is half buried into the hillside and offers a spatial complexity and informality that some critics have seen as drawing on the work of Frank Lloyd Wright. But it supports a way of life that is more like *Swallows and Amazons*.

Living and dining rooms are contained in a two-storey, split-level space; the elevation facing the sea is completely glazed. A lower, single-storey wing provides bedroom accommodation, with the two wings of the house cut in half by an outdoor path that takes you from the access road, across a bridge, past the front door, and then tumbles down a cascade of grassed steps towards the garden.

The details of Creak Vean's design have been echoed in later projects by Team 4's various former members. The kitchen, for example, with its stainless-steel island work bench, has a marked resemblance to Rogers's own kitchen in Chelsea, where the fashionable River Café was born (the house was completed in 1985). Here and there are traces of Rogers's predilection for vivid colour. There are also signals of what was to become Norman Foster's passion for simplified geometric form. The way the entrance bridge approaches the front door at an oblique angle, for example, recalls the tentative way that Foster designed the entrance to the Sainsbury Centre for Visual Arts at the University of East Anglia, in 1978.

Creak Vean was built at a moment when Britain was discovering the pleasures of hedonism, and was running out of patience with old conventions. Moral values were revolutionized – among much else – by oral contraception which was to have an impact not just on fertility but eventually on house size too. Affluence was propelling Britain from being a society that limited itself to six inches of bath water twice a week, towards the sauna and the power shower; from the coin-operated gas fire to central heating; and from the outside lavatory to the low-level suite. Substantial numbers of people were able to enjoy a standard of living that for the first time brought them the means to take a refrigerator, a television set, and a car for granted. When these consumer items were new, there was still a belief among their designers that it was important to treat household goods with due respect. They were expensive and they needed to look it. They were unfamiliar, and they needed to reassure the consumer that they were reliable. And they had to be made intelligible enough to communicate their function and method of operation without continual reference to the manual. This was also a period in which the world was still in a state of dizzy intoxication over the excitement of the possibilities offered by technology, a period when Harold Wilson made his famous speech about a renewed Britain embracing the white-hot heat of the technological revolution.

But as far as the social impact of consumer artefacts was concerned, what counted was not so much how the object looked, as what it did to the way the home was used. In the 1950s and 1960s, the television set assumed a dominant position at the centre of the home, a flickering, electronic hearth. Instead of gathering around a fireplace, the family would be focused on the single television set. As television sets became cheaper, an entire nation began to share a television agenda.

The result is that the television has dispersed around the home to make viewing an increasingly private experience (a dispersion made possible by the increasing adoption of central heating which made the whole house usable in winter after dark): children retreat to their own bedrooms with a portable set and adults watch television in the kitchen and even the bath. A similar phenomenon has transformed the meaning of other appliances too. The telephone is no longer marooned in isolation in the entrance hall as it once was, but has became available throughout the house. And it is no longer tied to static phone lines. And in the 1990s, the mobile phone has transformed it as a means of communication, no longer tied to a specific place within the home, or even to any address at all.

Robert Venturi's house for his mother was a self-conscious attempt to go beyond what he regarded as the impoverished language of modernity in order to devise a richer, more allusive architecture. Venturi's pattern of windows and his play between symmetry and asymmetry suggest a mannerist sensibility.

Vanna Venturi house

first floor

ground floor

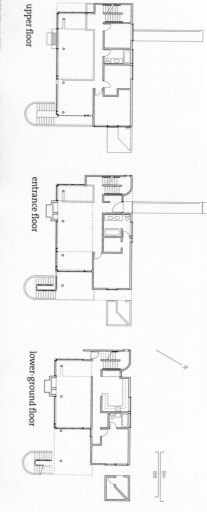

upper floor

entrance floor

lower-ground floor

Richard Meier established his reputation with the Smith house in Darien, Connecticut, completed in 1967. As Meier said, the design was based on a reworking of Le Corbusier's motifs, as synthesized in the latter's Citrohan and Domino houses. Unlike Le Corbusier, Meier was able to use giant panes of glass to define the facades of the Smith house.

Norman Foster and Richard Rogers designed Creak Vean as part of Team 4 when they returned to Britain from the United States in 1965. Echoing Frank Lloyd Wright, the house makes the most of its seafront setting and seems to emerge from the landscape. An external staircase cuts the two wings of Creak Vean in distinct halves.

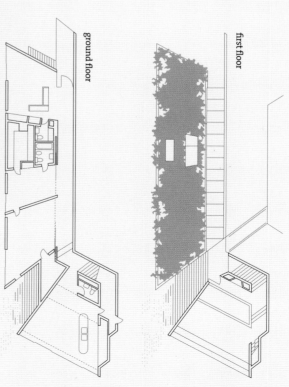

ground floor

first floor

Creak Vean

8

Seaside, the Florida holiday resort master planned by Andres Duany and Elizabeth Plater-Zyberk under the inspiration of Leon Krier, attempted to reconstruct the urbanity of small town America (top).

Peter Eisenman's design for a house in West Cornwall, Connecticut, was based on a dramatically different conception of domestic architecture: rather than a vision of nostalgia, it was self-contained and self-referential.

The American architects who had made the intellectual running in the 1960s – Richard Meier, Michael Graves, Robert A.M. Stern, Peter Eisenman and for a while even Frank Gehry, who was a little older, but would not really make his own mark until the 1980s – all found themselves overshadowed in the 1970s by Philip Johnson. The interaction between the older man and the younger architects was complex. Johnson had established a kind of salon that put him at the centre of a privileged group of architects meeting regularly for lunch and conversation, sometimes at the Four Seasons restaurant and sometimes at the Century Club.

It was a relationship that worked both ways. To be welcomed into a circle centred around one of the most influential architects in America was clearly attractive to a new generation seeking to establish itself. But there was something for Johnson in all this too. He was, as he had always been, looking to find architectural inspiration through the exploration of innovative new talent. Nor was he content to remain a mere critic, commentating from the sidelines, but was determined to build on his own account.

At a time in his life when most architects contemplate retirement, Johnson turned his back on the architecture that inspired the earlier part of his career, took on postmodernism and turned its aspirations for an architecture of subtlety and allusion to symbolic, emotional and poetic values into a cartoon language. Johnson looked at the domestic experiments of the younger generation and translated them to the scale of skyscrapers, grabbing the cover of *Time* magazine in 1979 for his

notorious Chippendale-topped high rise for AT&T on Madison Avenue. In the process, he leapfrogged the originators of the movement and took on a leading role for himself. He produced an unbuilt design for an artfully camp little cottage in Big Sur that went even further than Venturi in embracing the architectural vocabulary of the commercial house builder, as well as taking a sly dig at the earliest projects of his first mentor, Mies van der Rohe. At New Canaan, the original Glass House was surrounded by a series of further pavilions and guest houses that amounted to a flourishing crop of experiments by Johnson, exploring new directions in domestic architecture. He was followed in this by the originators that he had overtaken, who began producing increasingly flamboyant domestic palaces.

Robert A.M. Stern in particular set himself up as a kind of latter-day Edwin Lutyens. In the Hamptons and Colorado, and wherever the rich gathered to build their houses, Stern was there, creating a stream of homes that pandered to the self-regard of a new generation of self-made millionaires, in the same way that Ralph Lauren offered the instant patina of old money through his archaeological approach to fashion. Architecture adopted the trappings of classicism – in some cases in the most literal sense – and mixed an uncomfortable range of references and witticisms, continually elaborating plans. Robert Venturi, John Rauch and Denise Scott Brown's Brandt house in Greenwich, Connecticut, completed in 1973, and Stern's Ehrman house in Armonk, New York, completed in 1976, took for their

point of reference another historical moment: the art deco period. To the unsympathetic, this was architecture using history as a kind of dressing-up box, a frivolous trivialization. For those who were involved, it appeared to offer some of the depth and richness that had been missing from the over-simplification of the 1960s, and promised to bring back the sense of craftsmanship and ornamentation that had once marked out the cherished from the merely utilitarian. The whole movement had its apotheosis in Seaside (1978–83), the holiday settlement on the Florida Coast immortalized on celluloid in the *Truman Show*. This was a whole town that found its generating principles within a pre-modern idea of Main Street, comprised of picturesque vistas. It was in part plain nostalgia but it was also a more serious attempt to deal with the sense of loss of the traditional neighbourhood by the freeway and the mall. Within Seaside, Leon Krier designed one of his few built houses, a classically derived tower house, and it was his view of cities that informed its actual master planners, Andres Duany and Elizabeth Plater-Zyberk.

But outside America, there were other views of what architecture could be. In 1973, Mario Botta completed the Bianchi house in Riva San Vitale on Lake Lugano in Italian-speaking Switzerland. With its strongly modelled simple shapes, a tower reached by a bridge suggested a more emotional form of modernity based on purist geometry, but also an acute sensitivity to site. In Japan, Tadao Ando's Wall house in Wakayama, Honshu, completed in 1977, together with his Matsumoto house in

Ashiya, Hyogo, completed in 1980, set the seal on his own brand of poetic minimalism, which ran directly counter to the florid eclecticism of American postmodernists. In the context of the visual chaos of contemporary Japan, with its endless vistas of neon advertising signs, and its rampant refusal to accept any functional separation in its cities, Ando's beautifully proportioned interiors provided a sense of order and calm.

Frank Gehry first made his mark in 1978–79 when he completed the remodelling of his own home in Santa Monica, California. Gehry had an altogether different take on the idea of the end of the belief in simple-minded modernity. Gehry made visible the conventionally invisible, taking the apparently banal constructional elements with which his straightforward suburban home was built – chain-link fencing, sheet rock, stud walls – and turning them into the starting point for a new sculptural approach to architecture that made the familiar extraordinary. With this very modest innovation, Gehry was able to blur the distinctions between interior and exterior, resulting in a highly ambiguous form that disrupts preconceptions about precious and humble materials.

Frank Gehry's transformation of a conventional Santa Monica suburban house (1978–79) into a layered series of additions using everyday constructional materials was an important watershed in his career. Chain-link fencing and sheet rock are deployed with the sensibility of an artist as much as an architect.

Gehry house

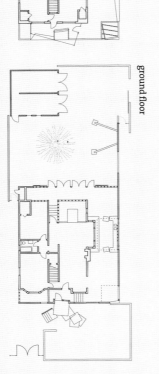

first floor

ground floor

Converted from a former warehouse in Princeton, New Jersey, Michael Graves has made his home (from 1974–92) out of a series of spaces of varying sizes and characteristics, unified by his interest in a modernized classicism. Both the interior and exterior have been extensively remodelled in a style that, while evoking the past, is clearly of its own time.

Graves house

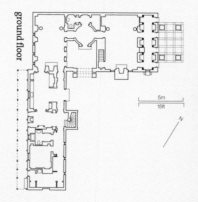

ground floor

5m
15ft

9

The rediscovery of complexity 1980–1990

Domestic architecture in the 1980s encompassed almost anything: from the severe austerity of Tadao Ando's minimalist concrete Koshino house in Osaka of 1981, which filters out the visual chaos of the contemporary Japanese city, to Alberto Alessi's house in Como designed for him by Alessandro Mendini in 1986. The latter acted as a kind of catalogue for the Alessi company's designers who were engaged in turning household objects – kettles, coffee-makers and cutlery – into design icons, and for its attitude to the new domestic landscape. In Japan, Ando struggled to find internal consistency in a complex and contradictory world, while the Alessi house celebrated an absence of consistency. The Alessi house is not the product of a single designer, but deployed a range of architects close to the Alessi family for various domestic elements and incidents, from fireplaces to specific rooms. It was a reminder that the 1980s were to be a decade in which the idea of simple, single solutions no longer applied, even as the pace of technological change grew ever more rapid.

The first Apple Macintosh computer was launched in 1980; the first compact disc in 1983: in their wake, the process of design, and the way in which design is visualized, were transformed forever. Instead of the plan – a conceptual tool of dubious value for the nonprofessional – there was the fly-through. And instead of the limitations of shape-making imposed by the techniques of conventional geometrical representation, came the limitless possibilities of computer modelling programs. For the first time, the client had a real chance of understanding exactly what their

architect was proposing before it was built.

But it was also a period of exploration in the language of design. The Carlton bookcase by Ettore Sottsass of 1981 had typified the Memphis movement, but there were other, even more transgressive ideas at large. London-based designer Daniel Weil abandoned formal shapes altogether and used a plastic bag to make a radio in 1981; and Ron Arad, also London-based, produced the teeth-jarring contrast between a diamond-stylus hi-fi system with a concrete base in 1986. Vitra put Frank Gehry's cardboard armchair into production in 1987. The aesthetic cycle was moving faster and faster: architecture was losing the sense of permanence that it had once been imbued with, and was turning into part of the fashion system.

In Eagle's Rock, Crowborough, in Sussex, designed in 1983 by Ian Ritchie for an elderly scientist, the elements of high tech were given a romantic new cast: an exposed cable-assisted structure put to domestic use, sitting in the midst of a lush green rural setting.

John Pawson and Claudio Silvestrin collaborated on the design of the Neuendorf house in Majorca, Spain, completed in 1989. It was a holiday house for a German art dealer that established a new direction for the domestic world – or rather adopted an old language and gave it new life. This was an architecture of simplicity that connected the refined language of Mies van der Rohe with the quiet dignity of a Cistercian monastery. It came as an appeal to older values of continuity and silence.

Frank Gehry, an increasingly significant figure, began to work

on a sculptural series of houses that foreshadowed his big public commissions in the 1990s, culminating in the Guggenheim Museum in Bilbao, Spain. The invention of his semi-expressionist Winston Guest House in Wayzata, Minnesota, in 1987, provided an indication of what was to come.

After a brief time lag, the language of objects went through a crisis of confidence that echoed the architectural hiatus of the 1970s. Ettore Sottsass in Milan played a similar role in design to that of Robert Venturi in architecture. Following a series of experiments and debates that involved designers such as Andrea Branzi and the critic/designer Alessandro Mendini, Sottsass created an approach to design that was as aware of history and emotional content as it was of functional issues. Under the name of Memphis, Sottsass gathered together a group of designers and issued a manifesto in 1982 full of overheated surrealism that sounded more like Dada than the Bauhaus. The point was to subvert the, by then, sterile conventions of good taste, and to replace them with a richer, more permissive approach to the design of domestic objects. There were strong parallels and a considerable overlap between architecture and design. Indeed, when Sottsass launched the Memphis group, he invited several architects associated with postmodernism, including Michael Graves and Hans Hollein from Vienna, to take part in order to add a wider international dimension to the project.

Memphis was an attempt to explore the greatest range of possibilities that design could offer: emotional as well as functional, playful as well as serious. Sottsass's provocations came at a particularly appropriate moment. The conception of design as following functional imperatives was based on objects that had already been displaced by microcircuits and anaemic beeping plastic. This transformation had removed the connection between form and function. A telephone, a washing machine, or a radio could be made to look like virtually anything, and still perform perfectly satisfactorily.

We have become much more attuned to the nature of objects that we use in the everyday course of our lives: the clothes we wear, the chairs we sit on, the computer screens we work at and the cars we drive. Not only because these objects have changed in themselves, but because we have become more aware of the whole range of qualities that such objects can possess. They are not, and in fact never have been, simple, functional artefacts. Consciously or unconsciously, we understand that objects have a personality. We value them not just for what they do, but for what they can represent and we look for possessions that reflect our sense of ourselves. We look for more than performance, but for objects that we can interact with: we buy an expensive 'diver's' watch not necessarily because we want to spend prolonged periods wearing oxygen bottles beneath the ocean, but because there is an appealing sense of glamour about the idea of a high-performance object, and an agreeable reflected glory in the sense of quality that comes from extreme precision. We buy a chair not just as a comfortable object to sit on – and in any case our perceptions of what is comfortable and what is not have a good deal to do with how

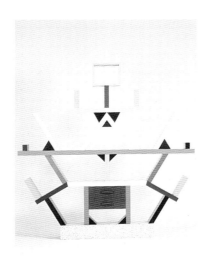

it looks – but also because it can express a sense of tradition, or of modernity. It can be a piece of domestic sculpture, or a means of giving a space a sense of enclosure.

Design in essence is the product of industrial production. It really only came into being when mass production broke the intimate connection between the craftsman who produced one-offs and his patron. Now that household artefacts are made in their millions rather than in small batches, it is the primary task of the designer to inject a sense of personality in the mass-produced object that the craftsman once introduced to the one-off.

The way that an object looks and feels can represent an enormous range of qualities. The finish, the way a control panel operates, the images that its form conjures up, even the sound a switch makes, can help to make the same mechanism appear expensive and precision-made, or playful and toy-like, just as the material used for a car's dashboard can project a wide range of not so subliminal messages about its pedigree: walnut means one thing, injection-moulded plastic quite another.

Initially, this was an unselfconscious characteristic. The first domestic machines were makeshift engineering solutions. The first telephones for example, or the early typewriters, were the result of mechanical solutions. Modern manufacturing techniques ensure that within a given product category, most brands at a given price will perform equally well. The job of the designer is then to differentiate one such product from another. And here the name of the game is product identity, where design is used to give products a personality.

A television set is not the precious status symbol that it once was. Now it is a toy, deliberately styled to look playful or nostalgic.

The designer also has the job of making clear how an object works. A product that can only be used with constant reference to a lengthy instruction manual is clearly a failure. The form of an object not only expresses what the object does, but also hints at how to operate it. As we have become more and more used to the culture of design, so we become more adept at understanding the nuances of the designer's repertoire. Once an object type has been established, the job gets easier. Follow the familiar language, and consumers will immediately understand which white steel box in the kitchen is the dishwasher, which is the washing machine and which is the refrigerator.

Koshino house

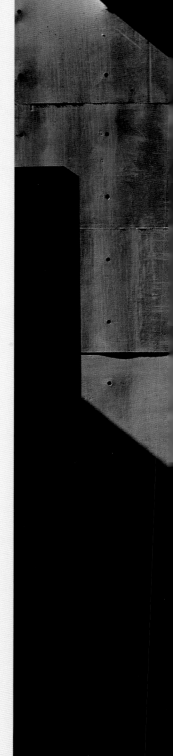

first floor

ground floor

N

Built between 1981 and 1984, the Koshino house in Kobe, designed by Tadao Ando, is formed of three elements, linked by an outdoor staircase. The finishes inside and out are of untreated concrete. The individual house set in greenery is a rarity in Japan.

Designed by John Pawson with Claudio Silvestrin, the Neuendorf house in Majorca, of 1989, recalls the tradition of calm austerity that has always been an underlying theme of prominent architecture.

A marble basin provides a sensual accent to the interiors, in which possessions and clutter are hidden away. The house carefully frames the landscape, while providing a sense of security and enclosure.

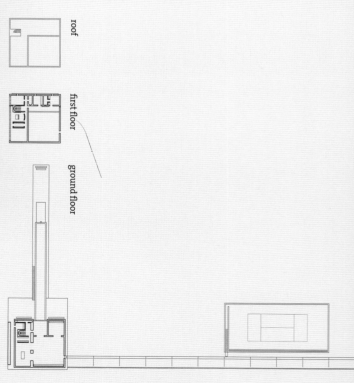

roof

first floor

ground floor

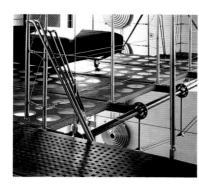

John Young, a partner of Richard Rogers, built his house on the roof of an apartment block in 1989. Its interior represents the apotheosis of the pursuit of the found object, as pioneered by Charles Eames. Young's bathroom (main picture, left) is formed out of glass bricks. The discs on the walls, commonly used in industrial processes, provide heating (top and far left). A sleeping platform floats on a mezzanine above the main living space (below).

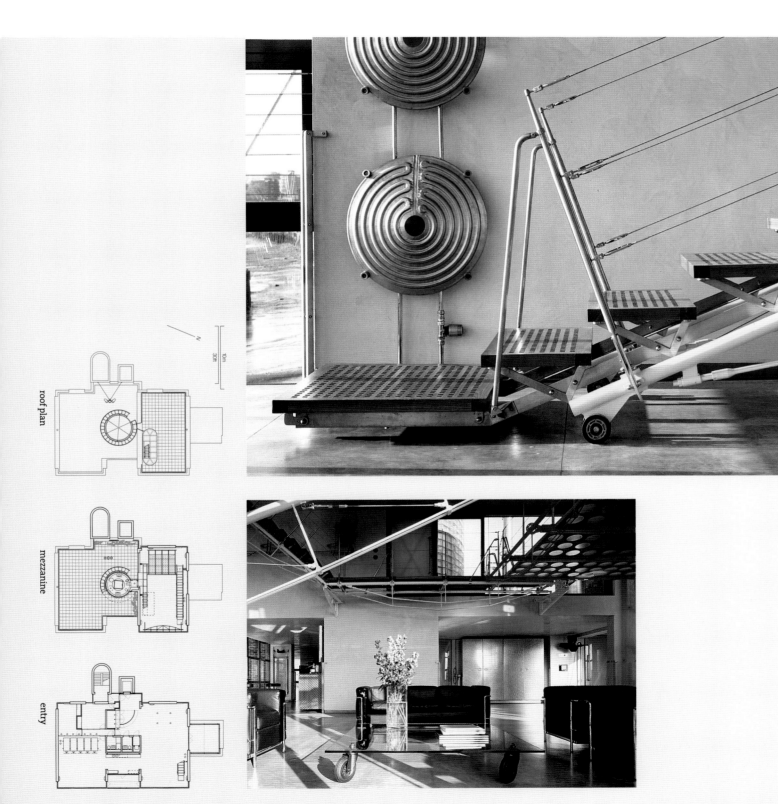

roof plan

mezzanine

entry

The private future
1990–2000

Rem Koolhaas's
Villa dall'Ava in the
Parisian suburb of
St Cloud, of 1991 (top);
Philippe Starck's
toothbrush for
L'Oréal/Goupil
Laboratories, France,
of 1990 (below).

The fall at the end of 1998 of the British politician who might well have become prime minister – the Minister for Trade and Industry, Peter Mandelson – tells us a great deal about the continuing significance of the house even in the mercurial world of contemporary politics. Here was one of the most politically adroit and astute men of his generation who lost everything in his chosen career for the sake of a house. In particular for an unwise loan to pay for the house. And what a house. An inner-city white-stucco mid-nineteenth-century terraced house, which in the hands of Mandelson's designer Steth Stein – 'society architect' as one London critic described him – was transformed into a residence suitable for a cabinet minister, a man of influence, and a man of affairs. It was always a house high on symbolism: it had a kitchen, but Mandelson never cooked in it. It was big enough to house a family and its servants but Mandelson never had any intention of having either. And yet as Mandelson said, he borrowed the money he needed to buy it from his political ally Geoffrey Robinson so that he could be settled in his own home before the election of 1997. Here is the house as trophy, designed as a stage set on which the political transformation of Britain could be played out. Despite its miniature scale, it could have been Blenheim, or Monticello, or any of a score of politically significant houses of the past.

The dream of domesticity becomes more significant than its substance: the family-unit collapses, while fast food and restaurant culture, the microwave and the television, destroy the traditional

The Villa Wilbrink of
1992–94, by van Berkel
& Bos, exhibits Dutch
rationalism, but is still
an individual house (top).
Matteo Thun's kit house
is available off-the-peg,
and is tailored to a variety
of sites and sizes (below).

domestic focus of the home. The dining table becomes less and less significant, more and more of a formal prop. Even the kitchen, which had become a surrogate living room in the 1970s, turns into a trophy, full of high-powered equipment that is only for show. Stylistically, this is the age of irony, characterized by the sampling and recycling of the very recent past. We watch as endless streams of television chefs slip effortlessly from wok to bain-marie. The humblest supermarkets are stuffed with limitless varieties of focaccia bread and virgin olive oil. But at home, the nearest we get to gastronomy is the sacred copy of the *River Café Cook Book*. That and a preference for heating soup that comes from a cardboard carton rather than a tin can.

As if to assuage the feelings of inadequacy at this mismatch between aspiration and reality, we binge like bulimics, not so much on food, but on kitchen equipment. In one generation, the modest domestic stove has expanded into a top-of-the-line restaurant range large enough for a short-order cook to keep an entire diner happy. What does it matter if it is never put to work on anything more demanding than heating up the occasional cafetière?

In an effort to enforce the domestic dream, both Habitat and IKEA have based their stores on the creation of room settings that show, or teach, the consumer how to furnish a complete interior. Inevitably, both brand names have become strongly identified with a particular stylistic approach. With branches in a surrealistic variety of locations – including Beijing, Gateshead, Hong Kong, Kuala Lumpur, Madrid, New York

and Warsaw – and supplied from vast factories (many of them in the low-wage economies of Eastern Europe), IKEA is certainly the first furniture retailer to reach the living rooms of the world, and also the first to go out of its way to overturn the cultural norms of the consumers it has sought to convert to its ethos. Through its PS collection, launched at the start of the 1990s, IKEA has almost obliterated the gulf between high design and the marketplace. Its products are all but indistinguishable from the new sobriety of designers such as Jasper Morrison and Konstantin Grcic, working for leading Italian manufacturers, and are available at a fraction of the cost. So competitive is IKEA on price that it feels confident enough to retain the Swedish names it has adopted for its products, and even to launch a British television advertising campaign urging viewers to 'chuck out your chintz', implying that rather than tailor its products to suit public taste, it would rather change the taste of the public.

As if to reflect this culture based on the appearance, rather than on the substance of things, the architecture of the 1990s has embarked on an exploration of design as a set of signs. Rem Koolhaas's Villa dall'Ava, in the comfortable Paris suburb of St Cloud, completed in 1991, is faced in corrugated steel that jars gratingly with its stucco neighbours and comes equipped with an Astroturf roof with a lap pool aligned on the distant view of the Eiffel Tower. Internally, Koolhaas avoids the traditional architectural language of space: rather than a conventional sequence of rooms, one opening into the next, or linked by corridors, in

the Villa dall'Ava, the living spaces blur one into the next, arranged on a dynamic figure-of-eight race track that takes in ramps and abrupt transitions. The main living spaces on the ground floor sit in the garden, screened by curtains and bamboo. The upper level is supported on deliberately transgressive spindly concrete columns that jut in apparently random directions.

This was a decade in which the house pursued two sharply contrasting architectural directions. On one side there were those who looked to make order out of chaos, who tried to create perfection based on proportion and detail. There were many routes towards this goal: John Pawson's restraint, the precision of Glenn Murcutt in Australia, the purism of Richard Meier. And on the other side were the increasingly flamboyant, sculptural experiments of those who treated the house as an inhabited object. At the close of the twentieth century, domestic architecture has never been a more permissive and inclusive subject. It is no longer necessary to belong to one camp or another.

Designed by Pauhof Architects – Wolfgang Pauzenberger and Michael Hofstätter from Linz – House P, completed in 1997, is positioned to make the most of its alpine Austrian landscape setting. Externally, the house has a concrete base and an aluminium upper floor. These materials are softened by the warm colours and timber finishes of the interior.

House P

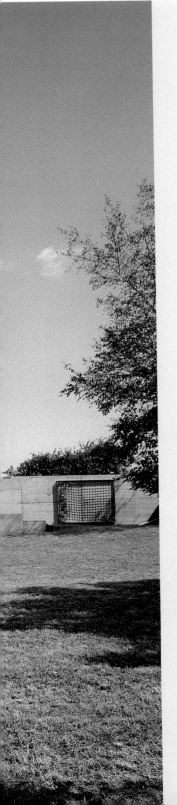

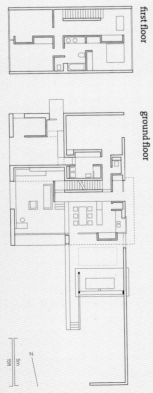

first floor

ground floor

5m
15ft

N

105

Rudin house

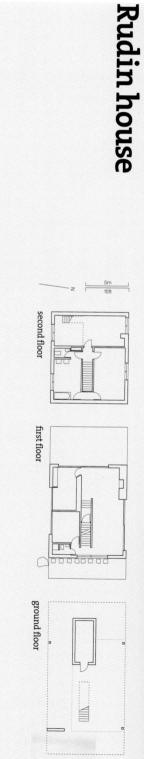

second floor

first floor

ground floor

5m
15ft

Designed by Herzog and de Meuron in 1993, the Rudin house at Leymen, in France, evokes childhood memories of what a house should look like: a big chimney, a steep roof and a single volume. The interior, with its raw concrete finishes, contrives to suggest an elemental simplicity, just as if the house had been carved out of rock.

The next generation: 50 new houses

Eychaner/Lee house
Chicago, Illinois, USA

Project team
Tadao Ando with
Masataka Yano

Construction
1992–98

The Eychaner/Lee house is Tadao Ando's first building in the United States. It exhibits his characteristic aesthetic restraint through the creation of a reflective, sculptural environment in a rich natural landscape. The site is abundantly wooded, but one tree in particular, a large poplar, much cherished by the owners, has shaped the house's design. In the midst of Ando's rigorous orthogonal geometry, just one wall is curved, to allow the tree to be preserved. Aside from the trees, Ando has introduced water into the house in the form of a pool.

The house itself consists of three distinct rectangular volumes. The largest, which is three storeys high, accommodates the family quarters. The second, half its size, is used for public spaces, which include a guest room and reception area. These two primary elements are connected by a third volume, which takes the form of a long and narrow living room. All these spaces are inward looking, and are focused on the pool. A ramp connects the pool with the second-floor terrace. This terrace, open to the sky, is the centrepiece of the house. According to Ando: 'The water surface is marked by the reflections of trees and the ripple caused by the breeze. This is a quiet space that introduces nature to everyday life.' The house uses a restricted palette of materials: the walls are exposed concrete, while floors are either granite or timber.

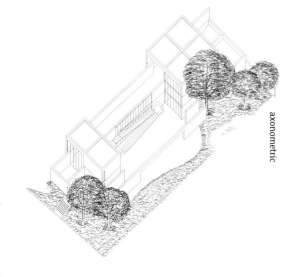

axonometric

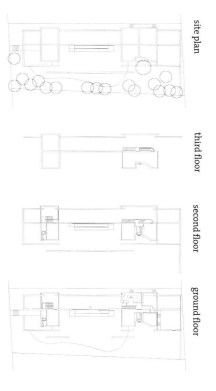

site plan

third floor

second floor

ground floor

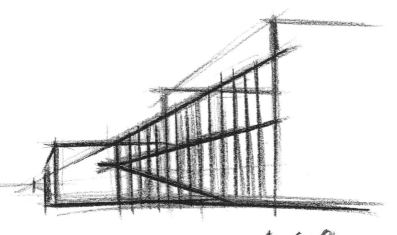

Ron Arad Associates
London

Amiga house
London, UK

Project team
Ron Arad with
Barnaby Gunning and
Geoff Crowther
Buro Happold: Mike Cook
(structural engineers)

Design
1997

Ron Arad was commissioned to
design a new house for the Amiga
family, a project that not only
involved tearing down an existing
house, but specified that the new
building would not mimic what
had gone before. The site is on a
quiet residential street that fringes
Hampstead Heath, originally laid
out in the 1920s by speculative
developers in a debased form of the
Arts and Crafts style. By the time
that Arad became involved, what
had originally been a cottage had
been expanded on several occasions.
The innate qualities it once had
were long dissipated.

Arad's clients were ready to start
again. They wanted to tear down the
property and asked their architect
to begin from the beginning. At any
point in the 1980s, this would have
been an impossible strategy. Britain
in the era of Prince of Wales's debate
on architecture was a country that
automatically assumed that new
meant worse: Arad's clients did
not subscribe to such a timid view
of the world. Arad proposed an
uncompromising design, based on
two interlocking egg-shaped shells,
which had nothing in common with
the insipid language of brick, or
pitched-tile roofs that characterized
the architecture of the area.
They were designed to be made
using a composite carbon-fibre
material, derived from boat-building
techniques.

The Body house
Cologne, Germany

Project team
Wiel Arets with Dominic Papa,
Sybille Thomke, Henrik Vuust,
Richard Welten,
Kim Egholm (models),
Wiel Arets (landscape)

Design
1995

sections

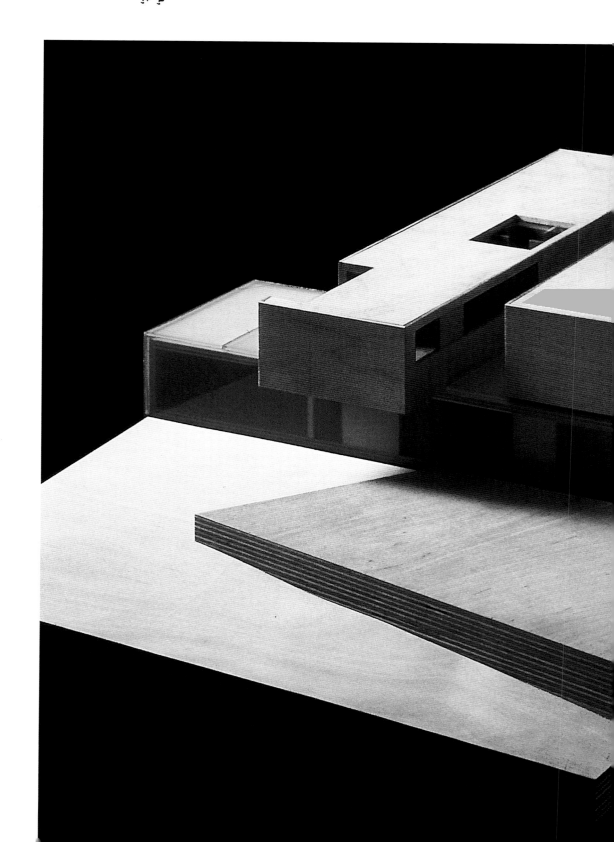

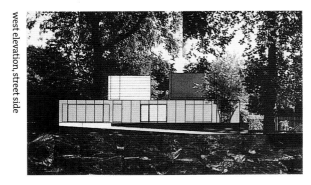

west elevation, street side

Wiel Arets Architects & Associates
Maastricht

The Body house was an attempt to design a villa with a more challenging relationship towards the landscape than could conventionally be expected from its suburban setting. The house was designed to allow a multiplicity of circulation routes to permeate it, creating a close relationship between the 'bodies' of the house, and the 'bodies' of its inhabitants.

The villa is divided into four equal parts that occupy the centre of the site. Its presence transforms the terrain on which it sits into two equal but distinct gardens: one is flat, the other slopes away from the street. The lower parts of the house connect and articulate the meeting point of the upper and lower garden levels to create a large fluid space where the family can congregate. Wrapped around it all is a continuous envelope of glass, where only the treatment of the material itself modifies the degree of privacy, enclosure, function and movement. Two massive stone volumes appear to hover over the glass envelope, each projecting itself into one of the gardens and providing a sheltered outdoor space. The family's private domain occupies this level, divided by the master bedroom and an area that serves as a guest house as well as the housekeeper's quarters. The simplicity of the basic volumes masks a complex arrangement combining privacy with carefully chosen views to the outside, and internal light created by the use of patios and skylights.

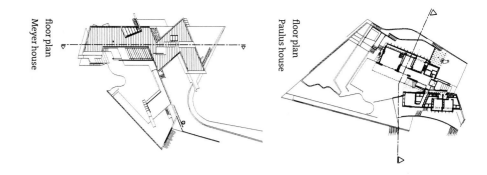

floor plan
Meyer house

floor plan
Paulus house

Conceived as a pair, the Meyer and Paulus houses occupy a rugged site with magnificent views over the southern Mediterranean coast of Spain, looking down towards Gibraltar. In response to the natural setting and to the domestic nature of the brief, the structure is broken up into a sequence of volumes that interact with the ground, the sun and the surrounding landscape.

The slope, together with the relative positions of the neighbouring sites, give the design of the programmatically similar houses two different orientations. The plan of the Meyer house, located on the steep mountainside, steps and unfolds downwards from the garage to the bedroom in a fan-shaped movement, reconstructing the original topography with a sloping unitary roof. The Paulus house, on a ridge, is based on the traditional typology of the patio house, with an introverted roof and a semi-enclosed courtyard providing framed views of the distant landscape.

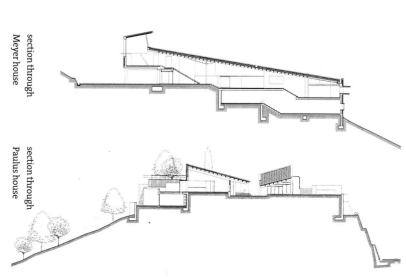

section through
Meyer house

section through
Paulus house

Alfredo Arribas Arquitectos Associades
Barcelona

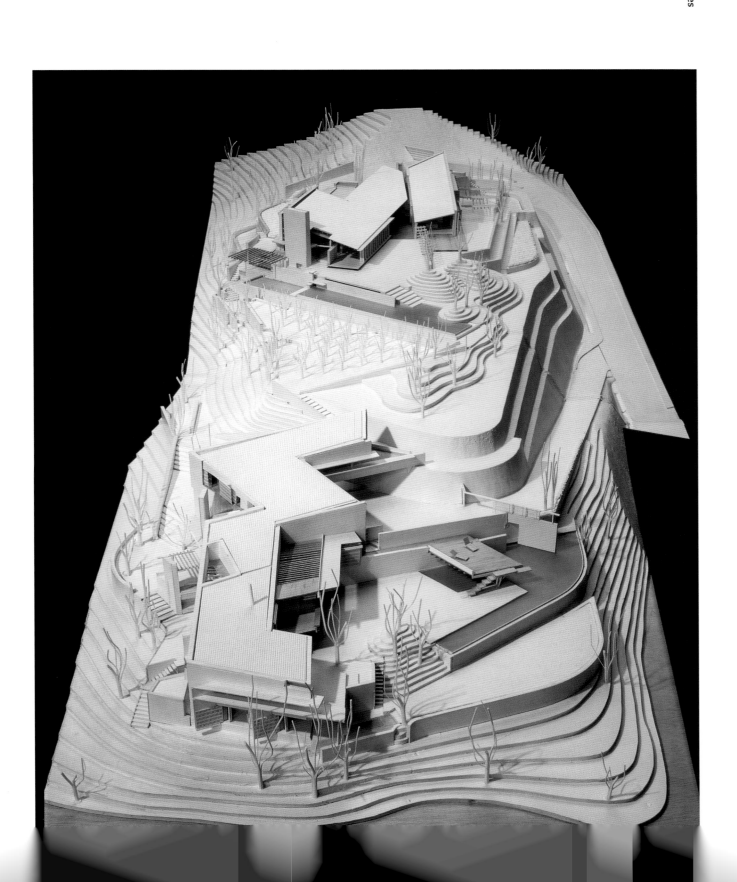

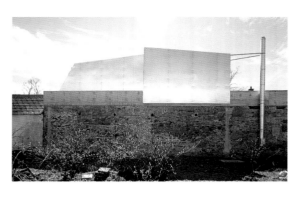

**Artec Architects
Vienna**

Zita Kern Space
Raasdorf, Austria

Bettina Götz and
Richard Manahl

Project team
Bettina Götz, Richard Manahl
with Maria Kirchweger

Construction
1997–98

This is an unusual space developed for an unusual woman. Zita Kern is both a farmer and a literary scholar, living on her family farm just outside Vienna. With a very tight budget, Artec designed a new home for her, formed out of an old stable. The new volume looks like a strange roof. Only the staircase seems to bring this aluminium-covered object into contact with its rough, everyday agricultural surroundings. The tension between the simple farm and this strange new eruption is spectacular. The space contains a studio room and two terraces. The bathroom is on the ground floor of the original building. The roof is designed to collect rainwater. The interiors are covered with rubber, poplar-plywood and aluminium.

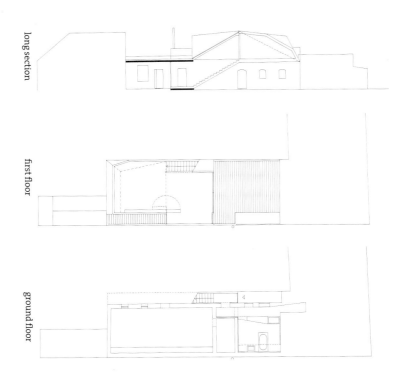

long section

first floor

ground floor

Shigeru Ban has designed a number of houses that are based on steel-framed glass cubes. This variant takes the form of a nine-square grid. The floor plan is a 10.4-metre (34-foot) square that allows for a variety of different spatial configurations, through a system of sliding doors and walls. With the walls fully extended, the plan is divided into nine identical spaces: the external walls to the north and south are transparent, and these too can be folded out of the way to open up the house to the landscape.

9 Square Grid house
Kanagawa Prefecture, Japan

Construction
1996–97

Shigeru Ban Architects
Tokyo

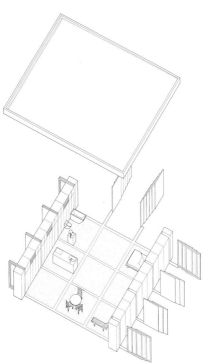

Ulmer house
Schwarzach, Austria

Carlo Baumschlager and
Dietmar Eberle

Construction
1997–98

Baumschlager & Eberle Bregenz

The Ulmer house is situated in the Rhein Valley in the Alps of western Austria. There is little space left for development in the main valley, which forms the primary transportation route towards the west. Consequently, most new housing development is densely packed together, leaving little free space between the houses.

Baumschlager & Eberle reacted to this problematic setting by designing a house that defines an external context for itself, rather than destroying it. The traditional division of rooms has been reorganized to create a more unified architectural statement which relates to the exterior, and allows for the creation of a larger garden area than would otherwise have been possible.

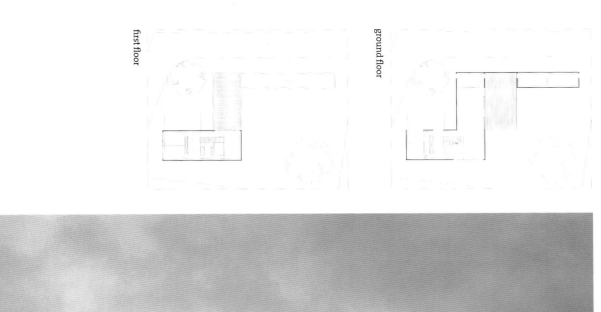

Detached house
Randers, Denmark

Project team
Susanne Hansen (project
architect), Matthias Hilgert
(3-D illustration)

Design
1998

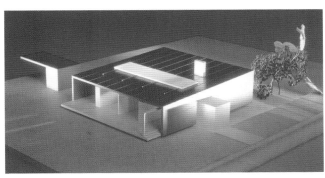

Bystrup Architects
Copenhagen

In an apparently small and simple box of steel and timber, Susanne Hansen from Bystrup Architects has developed a complex series of spaces. A slice has been cut across the basic box, running through the building from the entrance to the bathroom, both of which are transparent in themselves. This dividing line introduces natural light into every room of the house, and differentiates private space from communal living areas, without separating them from each other. Each room has its own view through the house, and allows for maximum flexibility in use. In addition, the rooms are designed with an external envelope that can almost be made to disappear, offering easy access to the garden, and allowing nature into the house. Specially designed furniture emphasizes the character of the house.

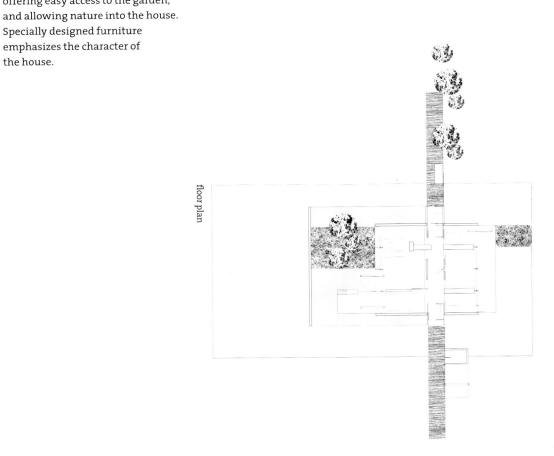

floor plan

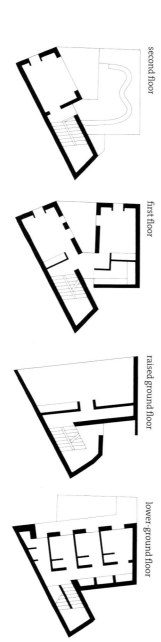

second floor

first floor

raised ground floor

lower-ground floor

Private house
Galicia, Spain

Project team
David Chipperfield
with Pablo Gallego-Picard,
Ove Arup & Partners,
Javier Estevez
(technical consultants),
Serinfra S.A. (contractor),
Tim Gatehouse Associates
(quantity surveyor)

Design
1995–97

David Chipperfield Architects
London

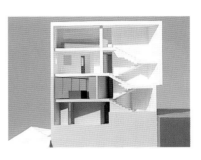

The house fills a gap in the main street of a small fishing village on the Atlantic coast of Galicia. The existing void offers a dramatic view to the harbour and the sea beyond. The village sits at the northern end of a large bay. The organization of the village follows complex geometries determined by the topography and the historical division of the land. The buildings along the sea turn their back to the ocean and face on to the sheltered space of the village. The form of the house was generated by a desire to resolve the complex site geometries and the heights of the surrounding buildings.

Some major openings have been introduced into the otherwise closed facade. The main living space not only provides a full view of the sea, but also defines the base and the top of the building. This base continues the massive stone and concrete of the harbour, while the upper part of the building takes on the same sculptural aesthetic. The stone and concrete base also give access via a stone ramp to the beach below. The street facade is closed, taking on the geometries of the street and forming a small entrance courtyard. The upper bedrooms are organized around a large enclosed terrace. This provides a framed and protected view of the sea, and introduces a hierarchy into the sculptural mass of the upper part of the building. The materials are concrete, stone and stucco and the windows are aluminium. All interiors have simple, white painted walls and sealed concrete floors.

Beach house
Playa Escondida, Peru

Project team
Henri Ciriani
with Enrique Santillana,
Jorge Draxl,
Pablo Gomez (engineer),
Francisco Barrantes (structural),
Roberto Ribeiro (mechanical)),
Jorge Angulo (electrical)

Construction
1998–99

'We are on the threshold of something new. This will not be an era of socially oriented ideologies but one of freedom from the implicit future. This situation presents all technological advances as highly desirable and is creating new spatial and visual conditions for houses... Our project tries to tackle this new approach. We are trying to concentrate in two architectonic directions: they both deal with space, one with the opening of enclosed spaces, the other the closing of open ones. These opposite conditions are reunited by setting the horizontal and vertical planes into motion, what we call "the continuous movement of matter".

'Typologically, this house is a cube whose base is a horizontally layered, enclosed centripetal patio emerging vertically into the centrifugally oriented upper volume, whose transparency is contained by a continuous concrete ribbon. By setting the central space of the house into motion, we also create an ever-changing panorama inside. To further this idea, we have covered the staircase with glass blocks, black mosaic and painted tiles in order to create a vision of industrial perfection as well as a pictorial one. These materials also enhance the idea of coolness one welcomes in beach houses. A palm tree follows this vertical thrust, manifesting the presence of nature in an otherwise all-mineral environment.'

The ground floor comprises the children's and guest bedrooms, staff quarters and a car and boat garage. On the upper levels are the living spaces, the master bedroom and, on the higher level, the solarium.

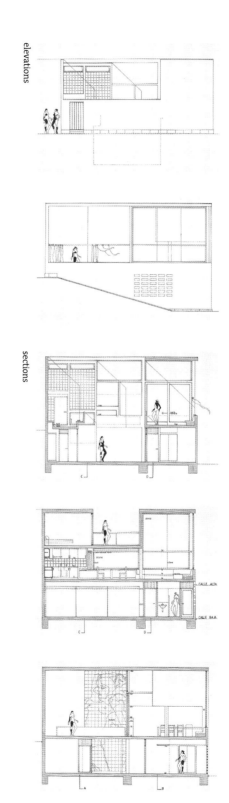

elevations

sections

136

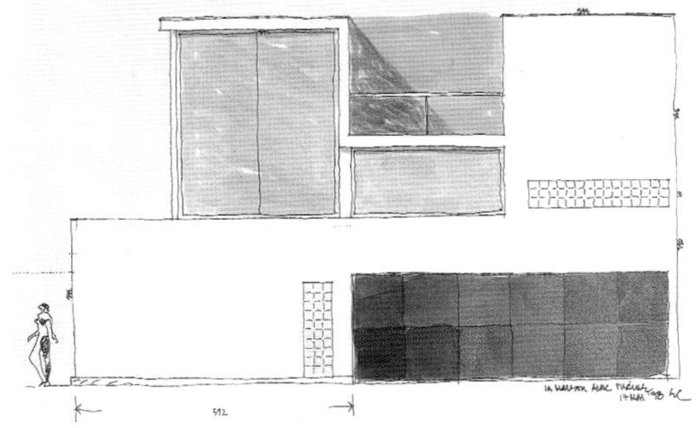

Henri Ciriani Architect
Paris

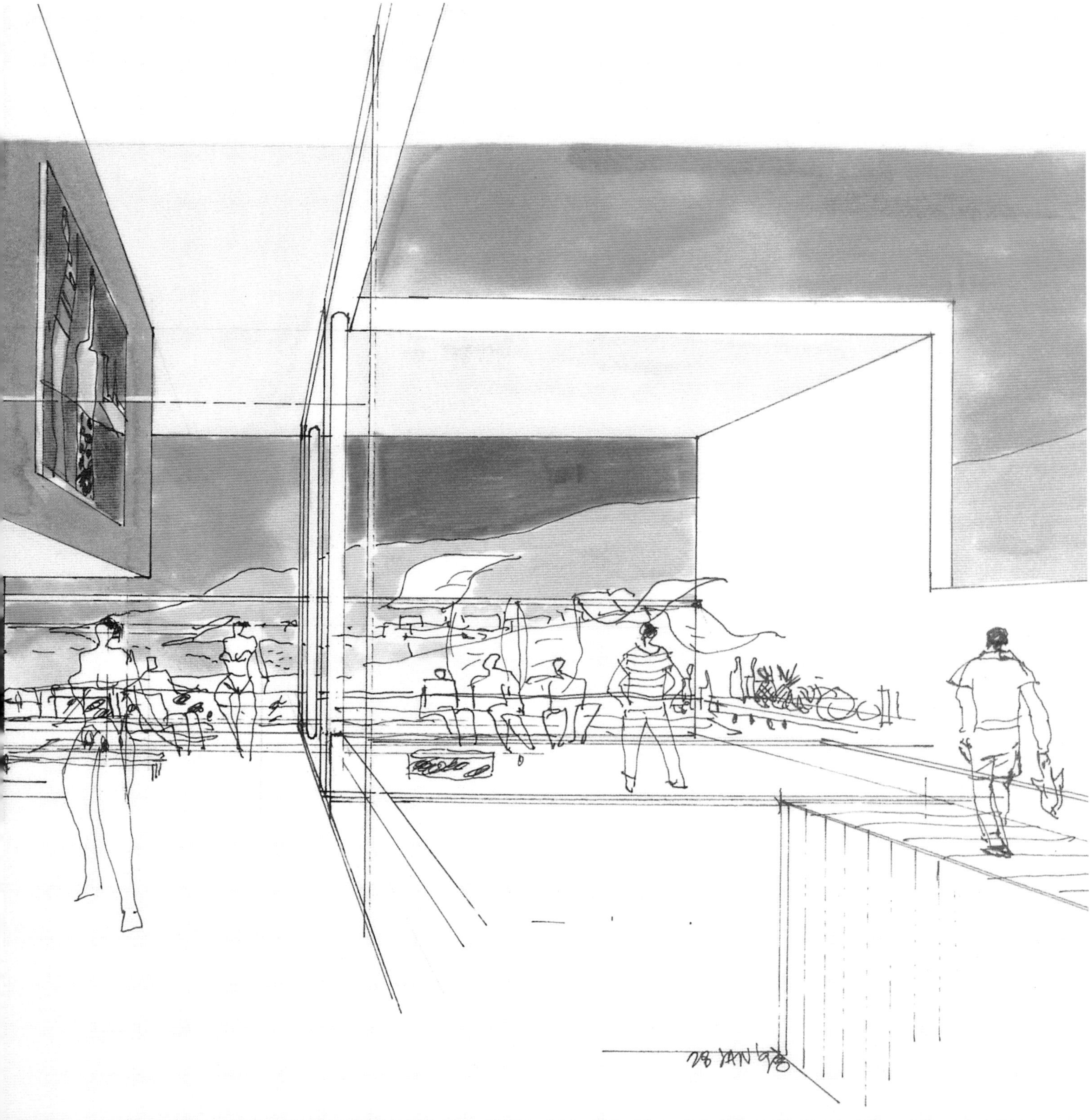

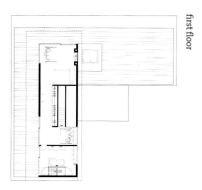

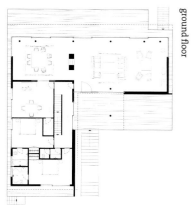

This L-shaped seaside house on Long Island sits on a dune and enjoys views to the Atlantic on one side and the privacy of a semi-courtyard on the other. The house shelters the pool, which forms the centre of activities. The construction is based on a traditional timber structure, with large expanses of glass to frame the magnificent views, creating an elegant yet casual weekend house.

Public rooms are organized on the ground floor facing the beach to the south, with the children's rooms and the kitchen/service functions in the adjacent wing. Parents' quarters are on the first floor, with access to the roof terrace and an outdoor jacuzzi. Long horizontal overhangs, fixed and sliding teak panels and open louvered teak canopies provide shelter from the sun. The use of vertical painted boarding is a reference to the traditional building type of the area, refined with stainless-steel edges. There is an additional guest house, with parking, garage facilities and private terrace areas.

Antonio Citterio and Partners
Milan

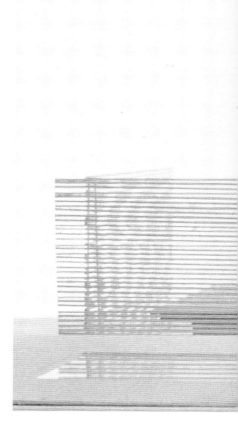

Weekend residence
Hampton Beach,
New York, USA

Project team
Antonio Citterio with
Laurence Quinn and
Patricia Viel

Construction
1998

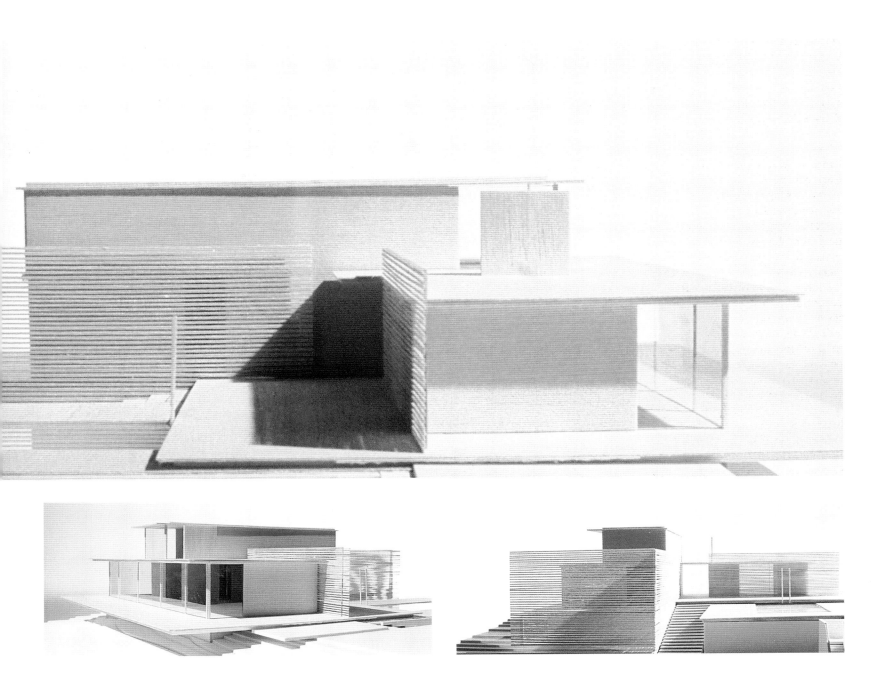

139

Villa Kerckhoffs
Meerssen, the Netherlands

Project team
Jo Coenen with Stefanie Hesse,
Danny Bovens

Construction
1998–99

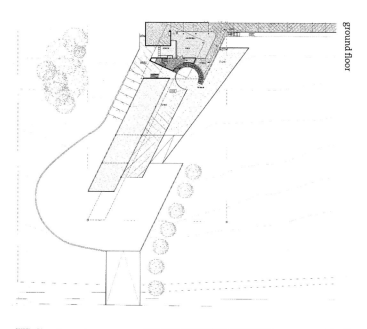

ground floor

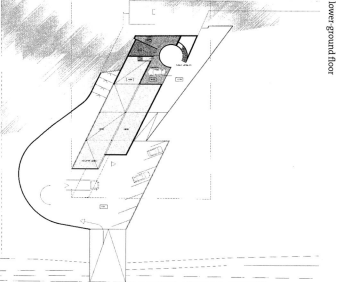

lower-ground floor

The site for the Villa Kerckhoffs, a rural area in the far south of the Netherlands, is subject to strict planning constraints. New domestic buildings are only permitted if they form part of a structure designed primarily for agricultural use.

To this end, the building includes shed space for agricultural machinery and produce storage. It also includes a small living area with big windows that offer beautiful views out over the hilly landscape, fulfilling one of the primary wishes of the client. The roofs of the house are orientated along the contour lines that run through the site at a diagonal. Two large overhanging roofs are used to emphasize the topography, and integrate the house with the landscape: walls are made of local sandstone.

The entrance to the house is at high level, reached by a ramp and a curved staircase. An informal path and a stretched pergola connect the surrounding orchards with the house, which meets the outdoors with an intimate sheltered exterior space equipped with an open fire.

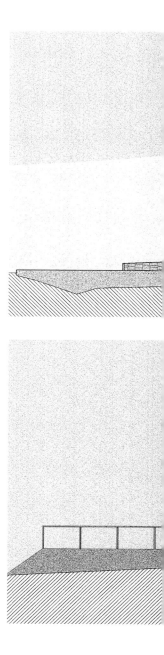

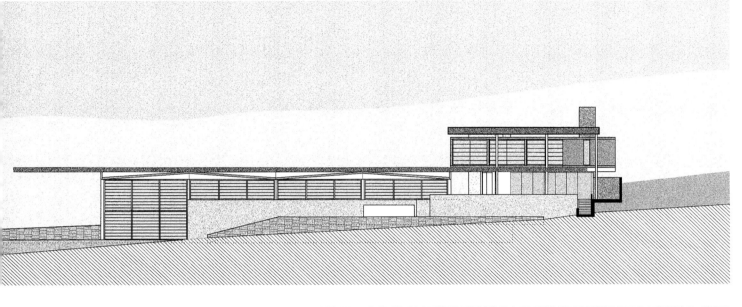

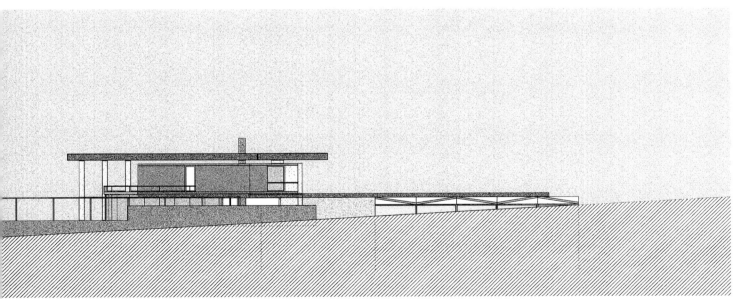

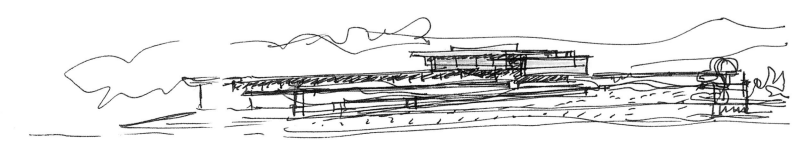

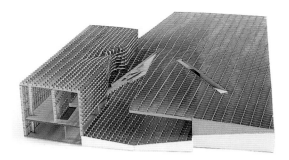

The house consists of two volumes which function as inverse proportional variants of each other. The extended volume to the front appears as a cast shadow from the main volume at the rear. As an inhabited landscape, it extends into the surface of the site and allows the main part of the building to hide partially behind it. The front outdoor space is protected from the sight and noise of the road, and allows activities to freely flow between the inside and outside of the building.

The site itself consists of four interfacing territories: car court; entrance hall and studio workshop apartment; living room, dining room and kitchen and library and bedrooms. These territories are defined by a structural membrane and supporting columns, building up a relationship between the sloped and level ceilings and floors. Using a two-way glulam structural frame milled by water jet technology, structural ribs are fixed together, supported by a system of steel beams and tubular columns. The frame is enclosed in a wooden-concrete panel system, which is combined with panes of fixed or openable windows.

ground floor

Preston Scott Cohen
Boston

House on a terminal line
New Jersey, USA

Project team
Preston Scott Cohen
with Alexandra Barker,
Michael Samra, Mark Careaga
(exhibition graphic design),
Chris Hoxie (collaborator)

Design
1998

Cookson Smith house
Twickenham, Middlesex, UK

Project team
Edward Cullinan
with John Winter,
Peter Inglis, John Romer
with Joanna Pencakowski,
Derek Lovejoy Partnership
(landscape design),
Michael Popper Associates
(services engineer),
Peter W. Gittins and Associates
(quantity surveyor),
Gilby Construction (contractor)

Construction
1996–99

river elevation

Edward Cullinan Architects
London

The Cookson Smith house is located on a long, narrow site, next to the River Thames. The division of the site into an A-B-A-B-A module on a 4.8-metre (15-foot) and 1.2-metre (3.9-foot) basis separates free and filled spaces, setting up the order of garage, courtyard, house (out of three boxes) and backyard.

The structure of the house is a slender steel frame that produces a simple 'box'. A curvilinear line runs through this box, demarcating spaces within the house and holding, or rather carrying, the suspended service rooms such as the bathroom, kitchen, study, and the stairway.

The curved line is also picked up in the landscape design as level and material changes. Crossing the site lengthwise on a timber deck brings visitors to the entrance lobby; passing through there, the deck eventually ends at the riverside, becoming a timber mooring. Following this line, one can experience the change from the designed street side to the naturally formed river edge.

Materials used are a brick-clad wall to the north, glass, steel and western red cedar to the south and east, with the roofs made of zinc.

section

Sheep Farm house
Victoria, Australia

John Denton, Bill Corker,
Barrie Marshall

Project team
Denton Corker Marshall Pty Ltd.
(including landscape
architecture),
Bonacci Winward Pty Ltd.
(engineers), Multiplex
Constructions Pty Ltd. (builder)

Construction
1997–98

Denton Corker Marshall
Melbourne

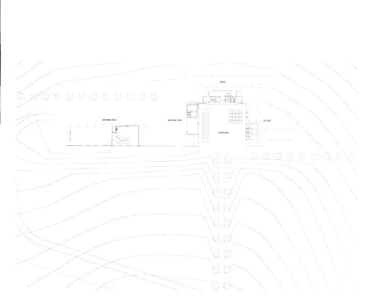

In the treeless granite hills north of Melbourne, Denton Corker Marshall has constructed – or, more accurately, hidden – a modern sheep farm for the production of ultra-fine wool.

The main house is a glass box with two smaller solid boxes incorporating the laundry, bedrooms and bathrooms. Approaching through a formal line of exotic trees (a common feature in Australian farms), visitors are confronted with a concrete wall that acts as a linking device to unify the various elements of the farm behind the house, machine shed, cottage and shearing shed. This single and austere intervention in the landscape shelters the courtyard. Behind an even higher charcoal wall, the actual entrance porch is both hidden and protected. After the discovery of the entrance, the view opens up to the house and farther on to the whole farm stretched out in the valley beyond. From the entrance area, covered pathways connect the house with the machine shed and the cottage. The buildings and the unifying concrete wall lean against each other, together with the sloping roofs which become a sheltering unity, structured in hierarchy from the main volume down to the shearing shed.

Donovan & Hill
Spring Hill

House C
Suburb of Brisbane, Australia

Brian Donovan
and Timothy Hill

Project team
Brian Donovan, Timothy Hill
with Fedor Medeck,
Michael Hogg

Construction
1991–98

House C is situated in a typical Brisbane suburb. The building sits on a hill and is entered from below. The landscape is used as if it were a stair that takes the visitor naturally to the centre of the house. In turn, an outdoor room that works as if it were the main square of a little village is sheltered by an overhanging roof and a narrow kitchen wing. Thanks to the mild climate, it can be used almost all year round by its inhabitants, whether an extended family, a single occupant, a couple, or an office. The house has the character of a miniature city.

Off-white concrete is the main construction material both for the exterior and interior, set off by a number of refined details. The concrete structure contrasts with the high level of craftsmanship. There are room-sized timber-framed lanterns, ventilation devices, timber joinery and infill walls, as well as skylights and extensive trellising for climbing vegetation.

Study for the house of
the deputy chef de post of
the Dutch Embassy
New Delhi, India

Project team
Eric van Egeraat
with Monica Adams,
Massimo Bertolano,
Paul-Martin Lied, Peter Heavens,
Stefan Frommer, Ole Schmidt

Design
1998

Eric van Egeraat Associated Architects Rotterdam

Eric van Egeraat's study for the house of a senior Dutch diplomat in New Delhi has to address two principal issues. A large part of the deputy chef de post's job involves social activities. He has to stay in close touch with Indian officials, businessmen and academics, keeping them aware of the economic and technological opportunities offered by the Netherlands.

The house has to provide the background for this role, but at the same time be a normal family home, a place for recreation and relaxation. This dual function has shaped the plan, which puts the public spaces – all of which have extensive glazing – on the outermost corner of the site, facing the front garden. Private rooms are on the first floor, overlooking a covered patio.

The key design issue addressed by Egeraat's study is the interaction between Dutch architecture and its Indian context. Egeraat's strategy is to employ new technologies realized using traditional building methods. Large roofs protect the house from the sun and there are sliding elements made of bamboo. Loose-laid stone walls function as sun filters, which allow the character of the interior to fluctuate continuously. In choosing materials such as grass, rock and water, the house becomes part of the landscape.

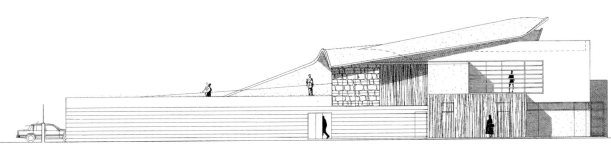

Engelen Moore
Sydney

The Rose house is a carefully sited square building close to a mountain and with a sea view. It takes full advantage of a north–south ridge on the site, avoiding the steeper slope so as to maximize the views. A light-weight steel structure minimizes the impact of the house on the landscape. The construction cantilevers 3.2 metres (10.4 feet) at the east and west sides. The floor is a concrete slab supported on permanent steel formwork, while the roof is light-weight steel.

The house is divided into three zones by two service areas. Parents have their own area, which is separated from a living/dining room, and in turn, from the children's part of the house. The two service zones pass through the floor to the ground level, concealing all plumbing and accommodating extensive storage areas. Covered decks run along the building north and south, providing weather and sun protection. The entrance is signalled by a louvred aluminium roof, which also functions as a porch.

cross section

long section

ground floor

156

Rose house
Kiama, New South Wales,
Australia

Tina Engelen and Ian Moore

Project team
Ian Moore, Tina Engelen with
Claire Meller, Sterrin O'Shea,
Peter Chan and Partners
(engineer), Cottier and Associates
(geotechnical engineer)

Construction
1998–99

The Dimmuhvarf house is on the edge of Kópavogur, a town close to Reykjavík, overlooking a lake and volcanic fields. Built on a sloping site, the house rises from a single storey to a two-storey structure on the lakeside. It is entered between retaining walls that provide shelter from what is very often a wild climate. At the same time, the walls signal the entrance to the garage. Half a flight of stairs leads up into the kitchen/dining area, oriented towards a sunken garden. Next to that is the bedroom wing. Further on, up another half flight of stairs, is the living room area, with an ante-room to one side serving as a study. Screen windows offer a magnificent view over the lake. An exposed concrete ceiling oversails the two levels, creating a distinctive space in this otherwise compact dwelling. Except for the in situ wall dividing the two levels of the building, the walls are plaster offset with mahogany and aluminium fittings.

Externally, the house is clad mainly in vertically corrugated copper with flat-seamed copper demarcating the entrance and clerestory lights. The roof is planted with the same vegetation as was originally on the site and will be allowed to return to a wild state. The intention is that the building will eventually blend into the landscape, as the copper oxidizes, and the grass grows on the roof.

Studio Granda
Reykjavík

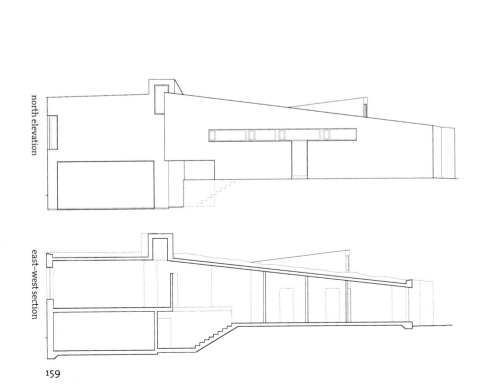

Dimmuhvarf house
Kópavogur, Iceland

Steve Christer and
Margret Hardardottir

Project team
Steve Christer with Gunnar
Bergmann Stefánsson,
Thorgeir Thorgeirsson
(structure and piped services),
Verkfraedisofan Jóhanns
Indridasonar (electrical services),
Ingvar & Kristján (concrete),
Páll Stefánsson (electrical
contractor), Örn Hafsteinnsson
(plumber), Gípsmúr – Árni
Thórvaldsson (plasterer),
KK Blikk (copper cladding)

Construction
1997–99

north elevation

east–west section

159

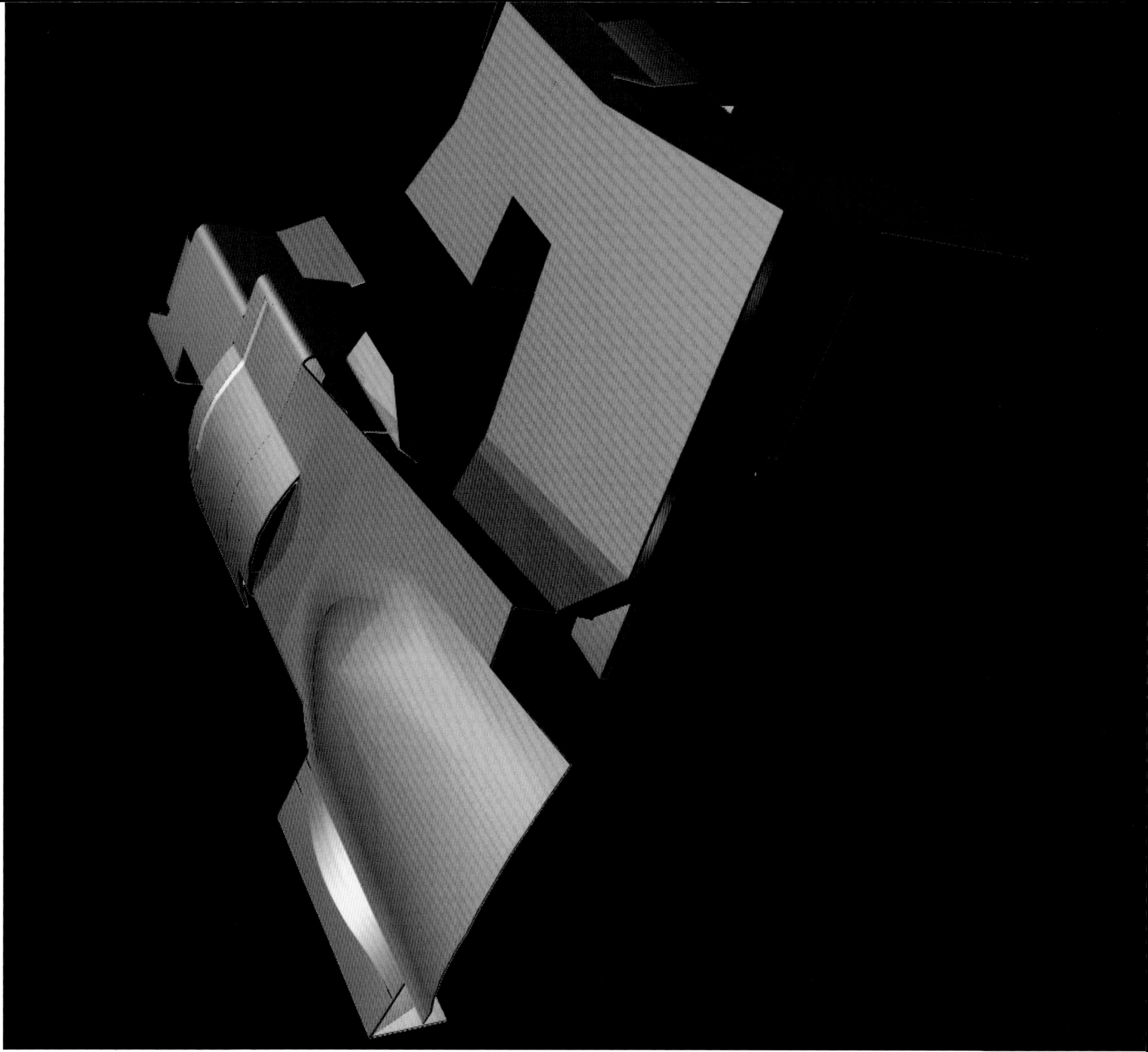

Oak Pass
Los Angeles, California, USA

Danelle Guthrie
and Tom Buresh

Project team
Danelle Guthrie, Tom Buresh
with Mark Skiles, Janice
Shimizu, Sophie Smits

Construction
1998–99

Guthrie + Buresh Architects
Los Angeles

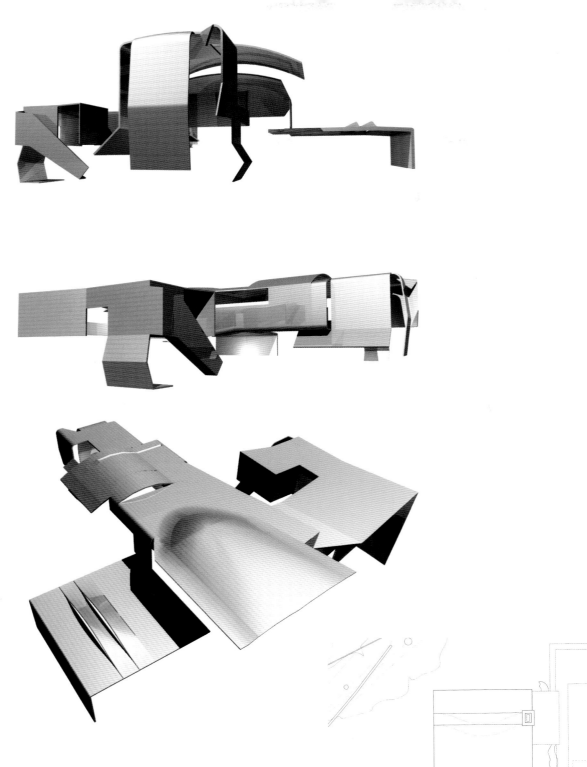

Oak Pass is situated in a clearing on an elevated wooded site in the Santa Monica foothills above Beverly Hills. The house will be the primary residence for a professional couple that has a keen interest in art and design, and their daughter. The project has developed over many discussions, various proposals and an extended period of time.

At the core of the work is the changing nature of the programme of the house in a domesticated landscape. The architects consider the relationship of form and programme to be evolving away from the 'tight fit' that characterized early modernism and wish to explore the potential of a 'loose fit' or even a misfit. Oak Pass recognizes the mutable domestic programme and looks to a more stable relationship between site, orientation and formal composition.

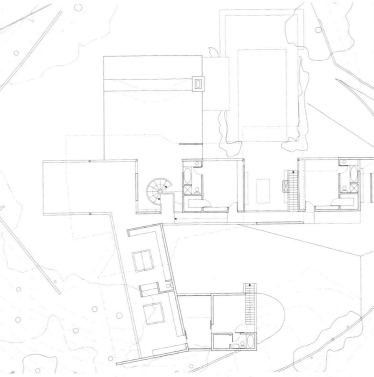

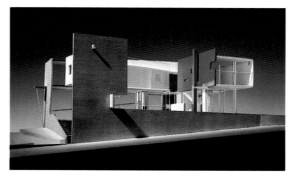

Hanrahan & Meyers Architects
New York

Duplicate house
Bedford, New York, USA

Thomas Hanrahan and
Victoria Meyers

Project team
Victoria Meyers, Thomas
Hanrahan, Lawrence Zeroth

Design
1997–98

This project explores ideas of duplication and the manner in which duplicates transform in response to the specifics of form, programme and site. These transformations are demonstrated in this house both in section and plan.

The programme is a house for a professional couple – a psychiatrist and a painter – with grown children. Both will use the house as a place in which to work as well as live. The house is sited on a south-westerly sloping wooded suburban area of Bedford, New York.

The first duplication involves a sectional idea of an upper building for working and sleeping. The lower construction is a pedestal that is terraced with respect to the slope of the site. The void between the two is a negotiated terrain of living.

The second duplication involves a plan opposition between the psychiatrist's consulting room and the painter's studio. These two volumes, the residue of an upper plate, are situated at the opposite sides of an open court.

The third duplication involves exterior walls, one red and one blue, that identify and transform the two workspaces. The duplication of these two walls suggests change over time. The walls sit at right angles and suggest alternative relations between the workspaces, the inner court and the landscape beyond.

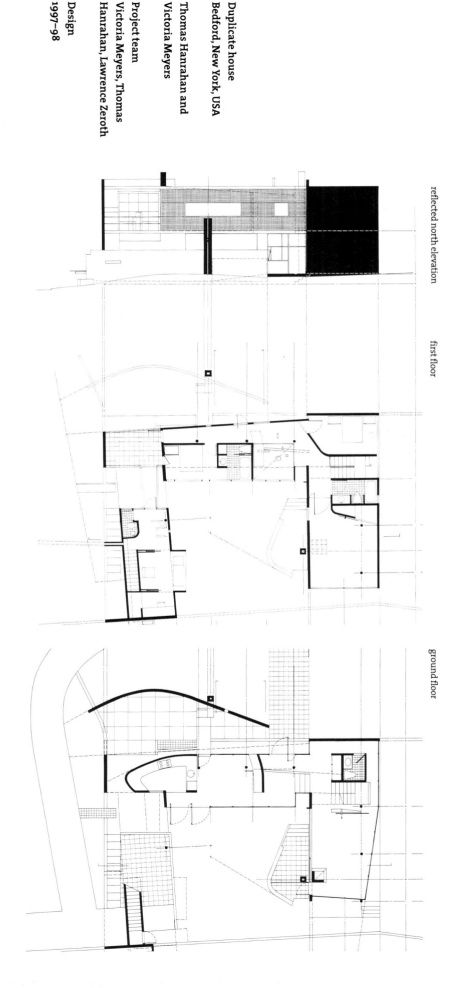

reflected north elevation

first floor

ground floor

Single-family house
Randers, Denmark

Christoffer Harlang
and Signe Stephensen

Construction
1998–99

Harlang & Stephensen Architects
Copenhagen

A modern interpretation of a traditional Danish building type called the *Laenge* was one of the prize-winning entries of the national competition in 1998 for detached housing development in Denmark.

One of the ambitions of Harlang & Stephensen was to develop a house with clear architectural qualities within the budget of a housing unit produced by the building industry. The architectural qualities of this simple rectangular building are more than clear, and are almost poetic, because of unexpected views and natural light brought in from various angles and sides. The organization of the house was kept deliberately simple to allow the freedom of choice according to modern expectations of family life: the centre room and the kitchen, which are considered the most important rooms in the building, were the only spaces provided for.

ground floor

first floor

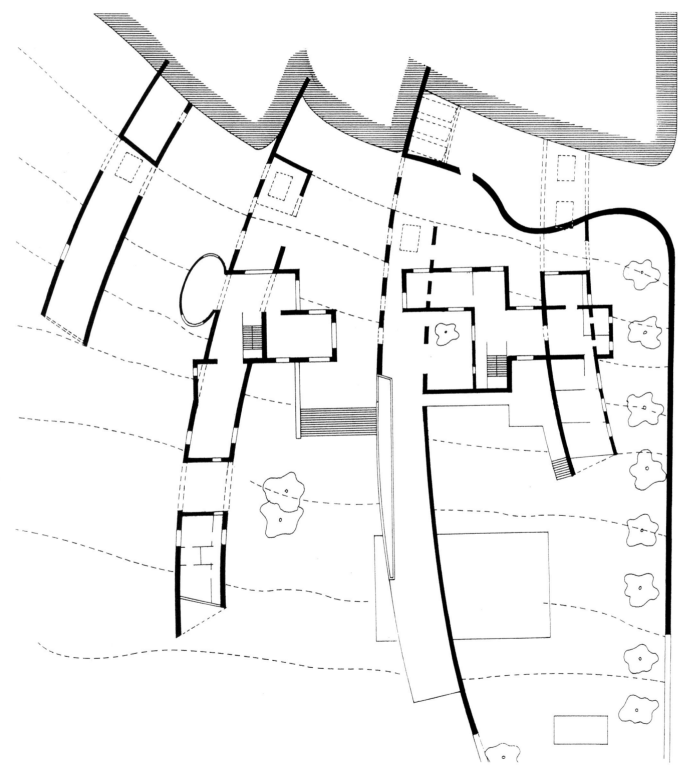

The Offer house is situated in an agricultural area outside Tel Aviv. The organization of the house was based on the way of life of the Offer family, with a central space for the parents, which is also the place in which family members meet and interact. The four children occupy a wing of their own on the eastern end of the site. The other parts at the far west of the site are changing rooms and service areas for the swimming pool and tennis court. The design takes the topography as its principle inspiration. The structure, while developing its own language, still reads as part of the surrounding landscape.

Single-family house
Vienna, Austria

Dieter Henke and
Marta Schreieck

Project team
Dieter Henke, Marta Schreieck
with Limin Chen, Rudolf Seidl,
Gmeiner Haferl
(structural engineer)

Construction
1997–98

Henke and Schreieck Architects
Vienna

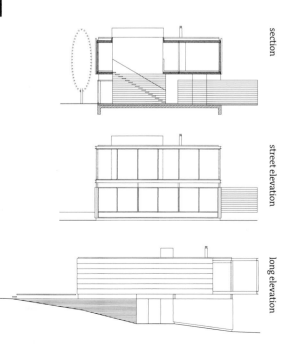

section

street elevation

long elevation

The house is located in a beautiful green area to the west of Vienna. Its position on the site was determined largely by building regulations. These restrictions led to the idea of developing a house that expresses a sense of duality, with an urban character facing the street and rural face opening on to an existing orchard.

The whole upper floor was designed to be a big single-volume space, structurally held by one retaining wall and cantilevering on the street side. The children's rooms were developed as independent boxes, placed underneath the upper-floor box.

Following the retaining wall, the house is entered from the long side. The upper floor is divided sideways by the staircase and lengthways by a long cupboard that splits the volume into different spaces.

The house uses a light-weight construction: the structure is made of steel while the floors and walls are of wood. Wood is also used for the interiors, resulting in a strong inside-outside relationship.

Single-family house
Asker, Norway

Hjeltnes & Pettersen Architects

Project team
Knut Hjeltnes, Hanne Pettersen,
Terje Orlien (civil engineer)

Construction
1995–97

Knut Hjeltnes Architects
Oslo

On a quiet site, not far from the Oslo Fjord, Knut Hjeltnes has designed a simple family house, working with Hanne Pettersen, with whom he was then associated. The calm location and a very tight budget inspired the design. The primary living floor consists of a single room that accommodates living, kitchen and dining areas separable by sliding rolling doors. A niche in one corner provides a children's hideaway which can alternatively be used as a guest room. An 11-metre (36-foot) wide window opens the building up on the south-eastern side, offering a spectacular view of the fjord. The second floor consists of four bedrooms and a bathroom. In this compact and rather modest house, specially designed furniture helps to provide an airy and spacious atmosphere.

As a reminder of the Scandinavian tradition, the interiors are characterized by pinewood floors and birch-ply partition walls, ceilings and kitchen cabinets. There are concrete floors for the entrance and bathroom. The plaster is coloured, the wood is treated with linseed oil and the roof is made of zinc, its colour intended to resemble an overcast sky.

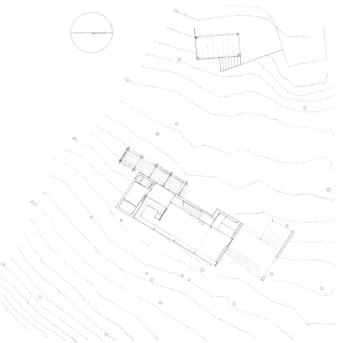

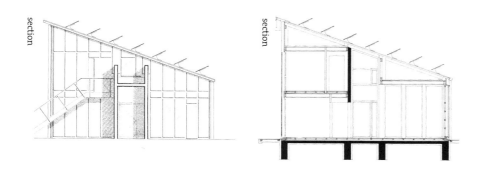

Mach house
Dessau, Germany

Project team
Prof. Johannes Kister, Reinhard
Scheithauer, Suzanne Gross

Construction
1995–98

Kister Scheithauer Gross
Cologne

The Mach house is built on what was once a nursery garden, and takes the greenhouse, a semi-industrial building type, as a major influence. The historically charged houses designed for the masters of the Bauhaus by Walter Gropius, with their Marcel Breuer furniture, are nearby, and they are another important influence. However, the new house answers its functional requirements in a completely different way.

The facade of the house appears as a free-standing concrete wall, but is actually an ante-room for the house, creating a series of pathways and small courtyards for the various inhabitants. The centrepiece of the house is defined by two concrete walls containing the main pathway through the house. The skin of the building is based on a wooden frame construction, clad with concrete panels, some acting as movable window shades. The roof is oriented towards the west and is shaded by wooden slats, mounted in a fixed position that allows the winter sun to enter the building and heat up the interior. As a result, the house is almost energy self-sufficient.

roof plan

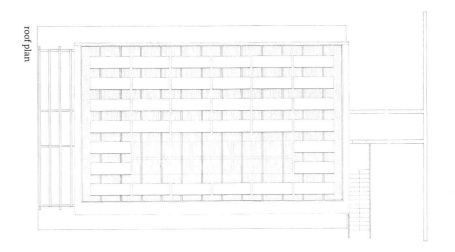

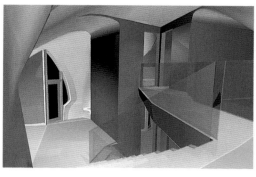

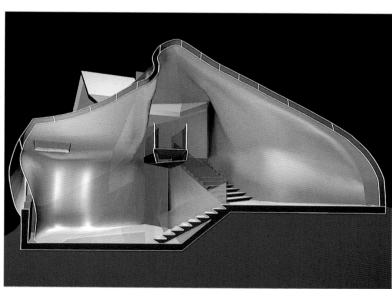

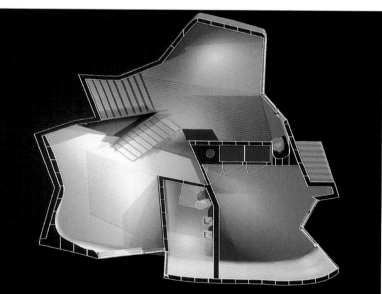

Kolatan/MacDonald Studio
New York

Raybold house and garden
Connecticut, USA

Sulan Kolatan
and William J. MacDonald

Project team
Sulan Kolatan
William J. MacDonald
with Erich Schoenenberger

Construction
1997–99

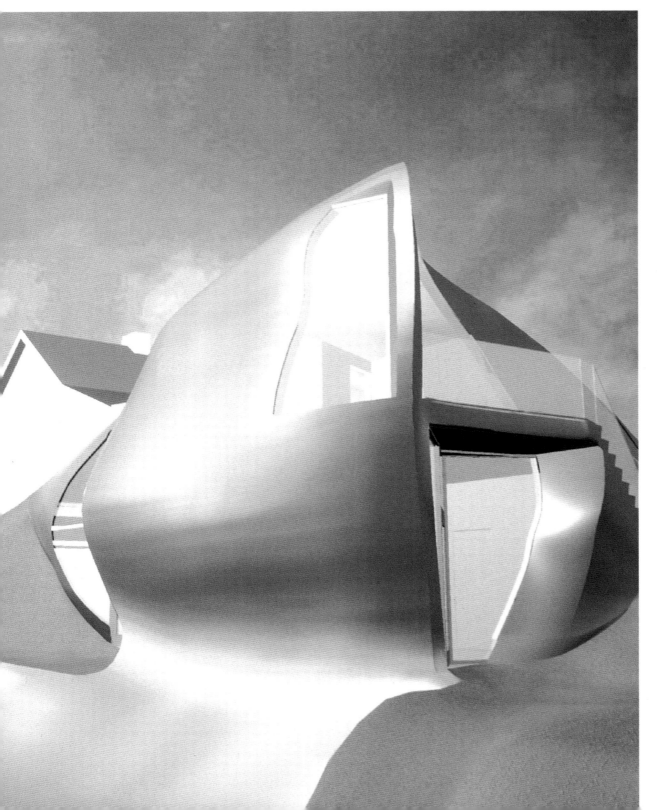

Existing structures on the site – including a pool, a barn and a traditional 'salt-box' house – are the cues used for the development of the Raybold house. But the traditional identities of these fragments have been transformed by a strategy that the architects call 'co-citation' and 'chimera'. It consequently has a formal, structural and systemic identity of its own, suggesting functions beyond their original meanings. The landscape is partially 'co-cited' in the new house and parts of the new house are now 'co-cited' in the landscape. Specific sites in the surrounding landscape are modified to take on a new identity, with clues taken from the house. The making of the house and the landscape are connected. Modified sites in the landscape that correspond to the house will then be employed as moulds for concrete panels used for both the surface and the structure of the house. When the panels are removed, the moulds will remain as part of the landscape. Concrete was selected as a malleable material that can adopt a wide range of formal and material identities.

House at Lege, Cap-Ferret
Bassin d'Arachon, France

Anne Lacaton and
Jean Philippe Vassal

Project team
Anne Lacaton
and Jean Philippe Vassal
with Sylvain Menaud,
Laurie Baggett, Pierre Yves
Portier, Emanuelle Delage
(collaborators),
CESMA – steel structure,
Ingerop Sud Ouest – foundations
(engineers),
INRA, Laboratoire de Rhéologie
du Bois à Cestas and Caue 33,
Mr Mousson, consultant
phytosanitaire (consultants)

Construction
1997–98

Lacaton & Vassal
Bordeaux

floor plan

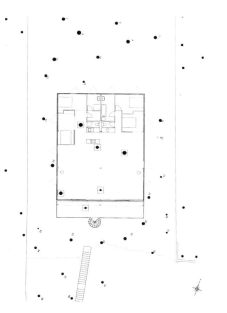

Lacaton & Vassal were asked to design a house on a beautiful untouched site overlooking the Bassin d'Arcachon, outside Bordeaux, without disturbing in any way the undulating landscape or the 50 existing pine trees. The result was a tree house, lifted off the ground and offering a spectacular view of the landscape. The house itself is a simple square box incorporating six trees, constructed with a steel frame and supported on piles between 2 and 4 metres (6 and 13 feet) high, depending on the topography. The view of the landscape is hardly disturbed, the piles visually becoming trees themselves. The facades and floor are made of corrugated aluminium, reflecting the water. Openings in the facade are made of corrugated plastic sheets. The elevation facing the waterside is completely transparent, made of glass sliding doors. Transparent plastic sheets, fitted to the tree trunks with flexible rubber gaskets, allow the trees to move in the wind.

Mack Architects
Los Angeles

Mark Mack

Thomas house
Las Vegas, Nevada, USA

Project team
Mark Mack with Tim Sakamoto
(project architect),
Ed Diamante (project assistant),
Eric Starin (associate architect),
Merlin Contracting &
Development – Steve Jones,
Bart Jones (contractor),
Morris Engineering – Bill Morris
(electrical),
Joe Kaplan Architectural
Lighting – Joe Kaplan (lighting),
Martin & Peltyn, Inc. –
Roger Peltyn (structural),
Southwest Air Conditioning –
Larry Halverson (mechanical)

Landscape
Bruce Anderson (design concept),
Anderson Envionmental
Design,
Hadland Landscape –
Richard Hadland (installation),
Brad Bouch (landscape lighting),
Jay Fleggenkuhle
(landscape architect)

Construction
1997–98

Under the burning heat of the Nevada desert, the Thomas house maintains the scale and appearance of shelter and privacy: a place of refuge and shade, away from the hustle and bustle of Las Vegas, the most mirage-like of towns. Located in a gated development, the house expresses the rigid regulations shaping planning in the area by withdrawing inward and suppressing the exterior facades. Like a traditional Islamic house that is organized as a reflection of its interior, the Thomas house addresses its exterior only as a collective street element. This is a traditional courtyard house that has been modified for the car-dominated society of the twentieth century.

The rooms, organized around an inner courtyard, represent a progression from the formal to the informal and the private. The house is approached by a hidden, almost Chinese, entry sequence of walls and water-cooling elements. The entrance, which is also a library, serves the formal activities of orientation and entertainment, while the kitchen/family room is an informal room for living. The rest of the house is private and secluded from both the formal and domestic activities.

The layering of walls provides an intricate relationship between the landscape and the man-made: their solid, neutral colours provide a backdrop to the more idiosyncratic colours of nature. Similarly, the large flying roof serves as a canvas for the changing qualities of light reflected off the water and walls.

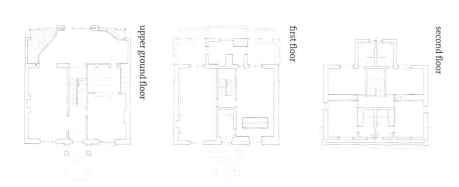

first floor

second floor

Private house
Hampstead, London, UK

Project team
Rick Mather
with Douglas McIntosh,
Charles Barclay, Gary McCluskey,
Richard Lindley, Chris Wisdom,
Peter Henderson Ass.
(quantity surveyor),
Atelier One (structural engineer),
Atelier Ten (M. & E. engineer),
Brooke Vincent & Partners
(party wall surveyor)

Rick Mather Architects
London

section

This commission was a rare chance for an architect to design a modern house in a predominately Georgian and Victorian neighbourhood. Considerable care was taken both by the client and the architect to consult on the design with residents, historical societies and the local authority. The new building, reflecting a 1930s modern tradition, fits into its context because of its reflection of the scale and materials used by its neighbours. The brief asked for a spacious, exciting 'sculpture' for living in, full of unexpected views and spaces, without being ostentatious. A pool and an associated room that could be used by the future grandchildren were part of the brief. The client's love of gardens and their wish for a close relationship with the exterior were satisfied by the inclusion of several roof terraces with wonderful views over the London skyline. Roof lights and transparent floors bring natural light into the pool on the ground floor and vice versa, introducing reflections of sun and water into the living quarters. Lying in the swimming pool, it is possible to look up through a glass floor to the roof light and the sky above.

Special attention was paid to optimizing energy use. Thick external insulation together with the pool give a large thermal mass, thus stabilizing internal conditions. Excess heat from the dehumidifying plant for the swimming pool is the main source for space and water heating. A heat exchanger on the ventilation system heats the incoming air.

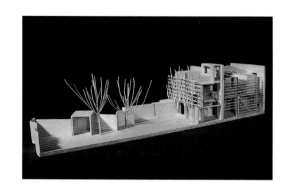

Enric Miralles, Benedetta Tagliabue Associated Architects
Barcelona

La Clota was once a distinct area outside the city of Barcelona. The city's continual expansion has now swallowed it, but some of the orchards and the original rural cottages have survived. Two of these cottages were amalgamated to create the Casa Trilla. The very modest dimensions of the existing rooms made it impossible to conceive of furniture as the means of making this interior habitable. Instead, the void, walls and the inner light of the original interiors will make the room habitable. Two houses have now become one room with a small garden.

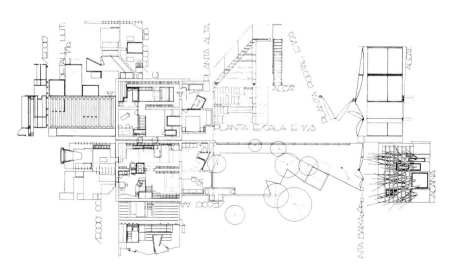

Casa Trilla
La Clota, Barcelona, Spain

Project team
Enric Miralles, Benedetta
Tagliabue (architects)
with Ricard Flores,
Nicolai Lund Overgaard,
Stépanie Le Draoullec,
Verena Arntheim,
Niels-Martin Larsen,
Ricardo Gimenez (collaborators),
Enric Miralles, Josep Ustrell
(construction),
Manuel Barreras (structure),
Makoto Fukuda (photo collages),
Kelie Mayfield,
Loren Freed (model)

Construction
1997–99

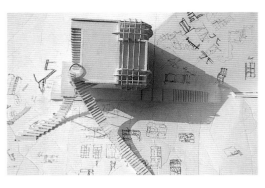

Eric Owen Moss
Los Angeles

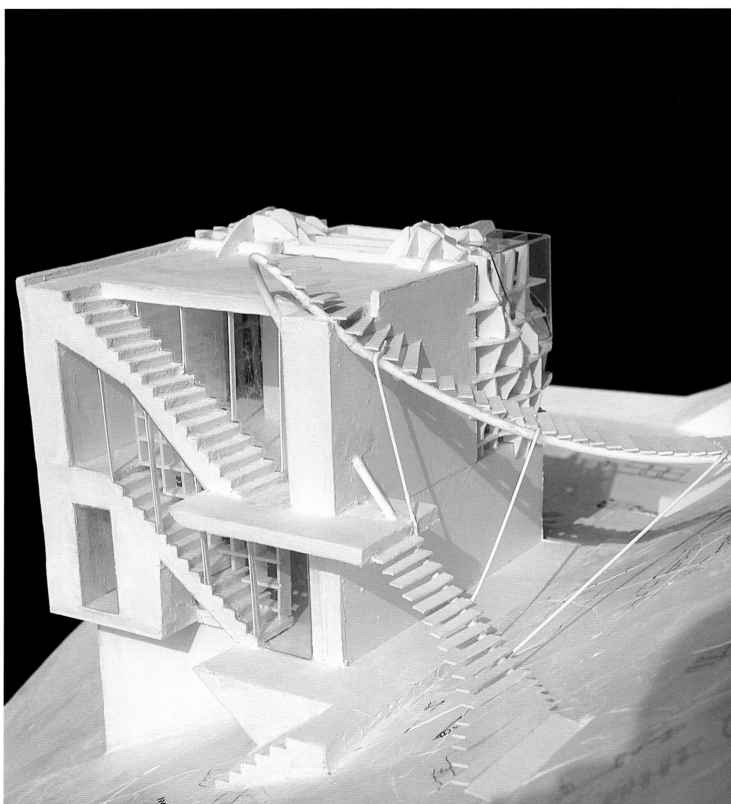

Mills house
'Un-boxing the box'
Hollywood, California, USA

Project team
Eric Owen Moss with Jay Vanos,
Scott Nakao (project architect),
Stuart MacGruder, Holly
Deichmann, Gudrun Weidemer,
Micah Heimlich, Corinna Gilbert,
Simon Businger (design team)

Design
1998

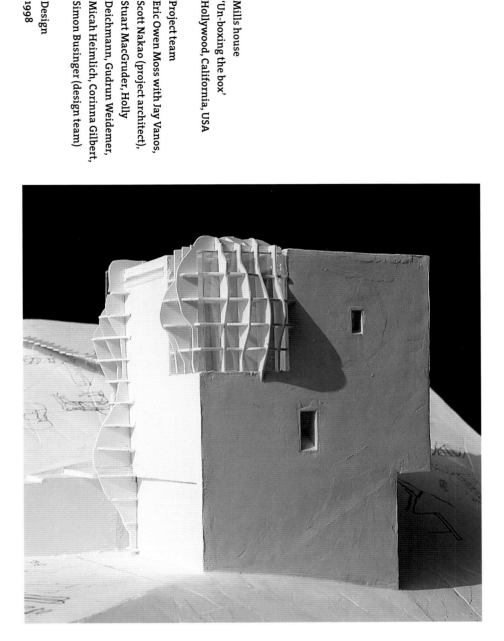

A young couple working in the entertainment industry planned to build a home within sight of the 'Hollywood' sign in the Hollywood Hills. The site, however – an almost unbuildable location – has a steep topography, further complicated by problematic soil conditions. As a consequence, only one portion of the site has sufficient horizontality to support a structure. A series of concrete caissons of up to 18 metres (60 feet) deep were drilled into the bedrock to provide the necessary support.

The costs of such an elaborate foundation, on top of an already tight budget, placed serious constraints on the design. These constraints dictated the discipline of a simple, orthogonal shape, essentially a box. To provide views of the 'Hollywood' sign, as well as of the surrounding city, the 'corners' were cut out, down through both floors. In elevation, the corners are a regular grid, echoing the simplicity of the box, but viewed in plan, the element is free-form, unpredictable and subversive. It is based on a curvilinear, egg-crate style construction: a way of melding irregularity on to a grid.

Two bridges, spanning from the first floor and the upper viewing deck to the side of the mountain, connect the house to the land, and provide views of the surrounding area. Plants and vines will be encouraged to grow on to the bridge, further rooting the house into the landscape. A curved steel pipe, reacting to the curve of the mountain, is the structural support for both stairs and slices through the house, once more disrupting the regularity of the box.

House on Bishop's Avenue
London, UK

Alfred Munkenbeck
and Steve Marshall

Project team
Alfred Munkenbeck,
Steve Marshall with
Charles Humphries,
Ray Thompson,
Tania Carlisle, Nickalls Roche
McMahon (structural engineers),
Fulcrum (service engineers),
Mick Mundy, Mark Laxton,
Craig Laubscher, Paul Sweeney
(Wallis Construction),
Northcroft (quantity surveyors),
Giancarlo Alhadef
(interior designer),
Isometrix (lighting design),
Jean Pierre Tortil
(interior furnishings)

Construction
1994–98

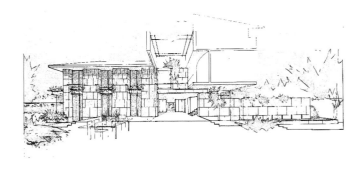

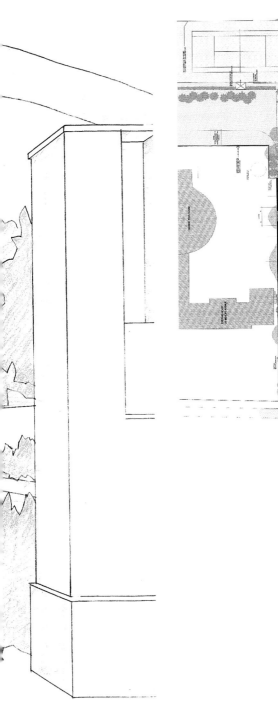

Munkenbeck and Marshall
London

Munkenbeck and Marshall had the rare chance to design a 1,858-square metre (20,000-square foot) private house in one of the most elegant residential areas of London, next to a golf course, on a site as big as a soccer ground. The firm designed a four-storey modern building within the restrictions of the Hampstead Garden Suburb's planning requirements, which are based on Arts and Crafts ideals.

A large sheltering roof binds the extensive spread of the house together, making it appear as a series of giant stone monoliths with wooden infills. 'The monoliths should appear as formal objects from another era gradually inhabited in an informal manner', says Alfred Munkenbeck. Materials used are steel frames with wood infills for the upper floors; the exterior of the building is constructed from Burgundian stone cladding and iroko wood, sealed to avoid colour changes. A pre-patinated zinc roof has wooden eaves, gutters included. The French windows are framed with afrormosia wood. The ground-level interior floors are made of stone; oak planks comprise the upper levels. The plaster is mostly polished Italian marmarino. The pool can be covered with an inflatable roof and a 'guillotine' window allows swimming between indoors and outside. A large Finnish sauna with a fully glazed elevation offers a luxurious view over the pool deck and the golf course.

Richard Murphy Architects
Edinburgh

north elevation

Next to the Huntly House Museum and the Scottish and Newcastle Breweries that sit at the bottom of the Royal Mile, Richard Murphy has developed a design for a house inspired and informed by the spirit of Edinburgh's medieval Old Town, but that takes into account the new buildings that are transforming this area, including Enric Miralles's new Scottish Parliament. Several features of the house refer to the reconstructed medieval architecture of the neighbouring Huntly House Museum, in particular an exposed external staircase leading to the front door, and deliberately down-scaled windows on the lower level that contrast with more generous glazing on the upper floor. Murphy has designed a building with a flowing interior plan that gradually rises up the house in a spiral.

The elevations are clearly structured by cantilevers, in particular the dining area, the master shower room and the large clear-glass living room window. The construction of the house uses traditional concrete-block walls, with the upper floor fabricated from galvanized steel and timber panels. These panels are of dark stained European redwood, contained in galvanized steel, and match the colour of the Huntly House Museum. The roofs are covered with Scotch slate and lead.

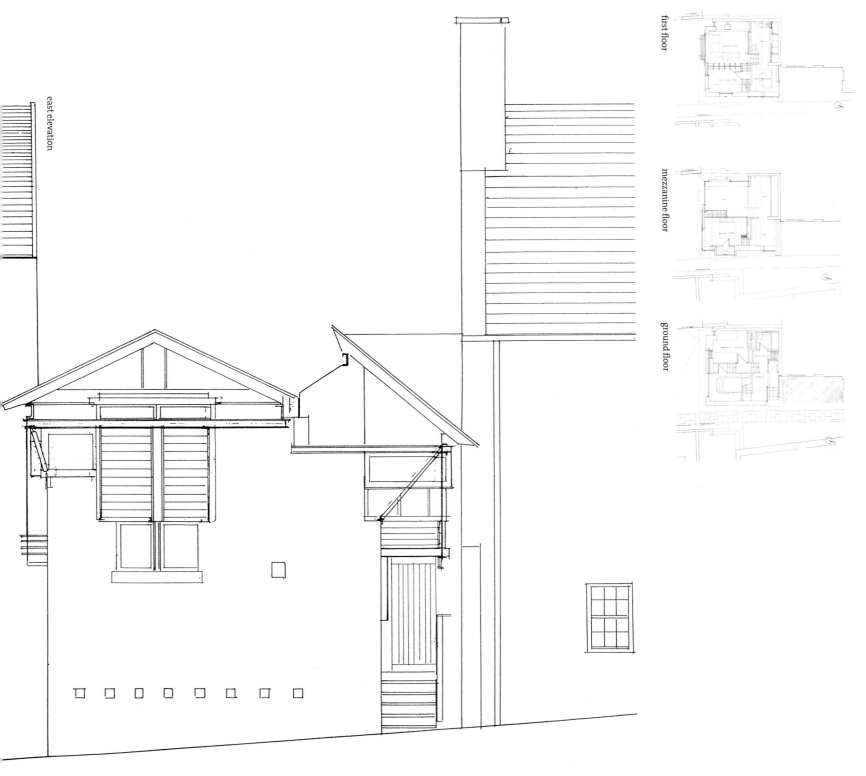

east elevation

first floor

mezzanine floor

ground floor

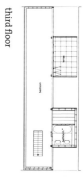

MVRDV
Rotterdam

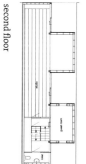

This pair of houses represents new Dutch housing development at its most extreme. Borneo-Sporenburg is one of the most dense developments in the Netherlands, on narrow strips of land in what was once the city's harbour. The architects have explored the potential of the site from an unorthodox point of view: to MVRDV, claustrophobia is not necessarily negative. Both plots are similar in size and location, and are near neighbours. Yet they adopt quite different approaches. One is slimmed down to the narrowest conceivable base, just 2.5-metres (8.2-feet) wide but 16-metres (54-feet) long, leaving an alley to its neighbour and providing the house with natural light from the completely transparent elevation facing the gap. The site is entered from a roof that slopes up from pavement level, allowing space for one car and a storage room beneath. Two enclosed volumes suspended within the glass facade incorporate the guest room and bathroom and provide extra depth for the two studios of the building.

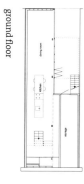

The other house is set on a site conventionally considered sufficient for three floors: MVRDV have managed to produce a design with four levels. These levels work as one continuous room: with the exception of two enclosed volumes, the garage at ground level and the closed bathroom. A series of rooms, differing in height and degree of privacy, are each connected with the exterior in their own way, ranging from a two-storey verandah facing the water; a balcony with a French window leading to the living room; a glass bay window to the bedroom; and a roof garden to the studio in the 'attic'.

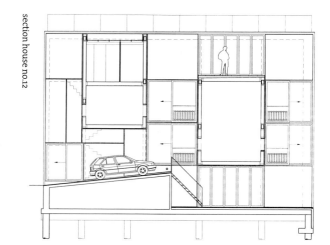

Two houses in Borneo-Sporenburg, No. 12 and No. 18
Amsterdam, the Netherlands

Winy Maas, Jacob van Rijs,
Nathalie de Vries

Project team
Winy Maas, Jacob van Rijs
and Nathalie de Vries with Joost
Glissenaar, Bart Spee,
Alex Brouwer and
Frans de Witte for No. 18,
Pieters Bouwtechniek,
Haarlem (structure),
DGMR, Arnhem (building
physics)

Construction
1997–99

elevation house no. 18

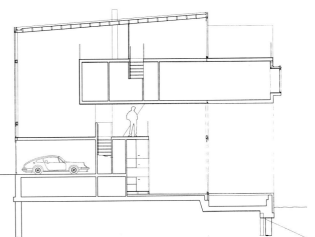

section house no. 18

third floor

second floor

first floor

ground floor

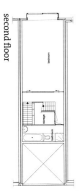

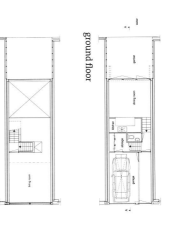

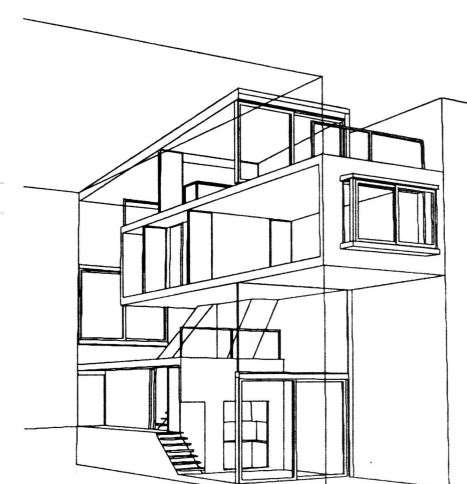

O'Donnell and Tuomey
Dublin

A narrow, linear garden behind an existing restaurant on Railway Street is the site for the Hudson house. The house was designed in response to the clients' particular requirements: they needed to be near to, but separate from, their workplace. Previously, they had been living over the restaurant and using an existing courtyard – the hollowed-out shell of a disused workshop – as an outdoor room.

The house is organized around three courtyards with external circulation between living and sleeping zones. The living space and bedroom tower are positioned on either side of the footprint of the former workshop. Storey-height retaining walls hold back the higher-level neighbours' gardens on either side of the court while the living-room roof is at the same level as the adjoining gardens.

The cast-in-situ cranked roof gives the living space a cave-like character. Glazed screen doors connect living and courtyard spaces and the stone floor runs from inside to outside. Access to the three bedroom floors is across the sunken courtyard. The upper bedrooms have views across the gardens to the Navan skyline. Concrete steps lead from the courtyard level along the side court to the existing raised garden at the rear. The house is built from concrete and lined internally with plasterboard and plywood. The external joinery is of untreated iroko.

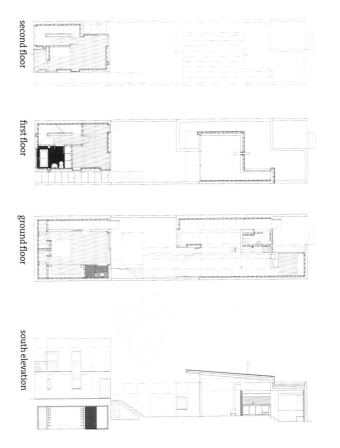

Hudson house
Navan, Co. Meath, Ireland

Sheila O'Donnell
and John Tuomey

Project team
Sheila O'Donnell, John Tuomey
with Fiona McDonald

Construction
1997–98

second floor

first floor

ground floor

south elevation

Shinichi Ogawa & Associates
Hiroshima

White Cube
Hiroshima, Japan

Project team
Shinichi Ogawa & Associates,
FIT (general contractors)

Construction
1997–98

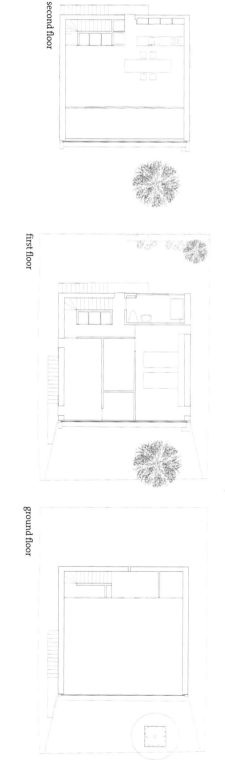

second floor

first floor

ground floor

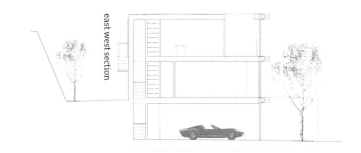

Shinichi Ogawa's reinforced concrete, three-storey White Cube measures 8.1 x 8.1 x 8.1 metres (26.5 x 26.5 x 26.5 feet), with a ceiling height of 2.7 metres (8.8 feet). Located in a suburb of Hiroshima, it is placed on a sunken space in the middle of the site. A shutter on the east face of each floor offers a degree of privacy. The garage occupies the ground level; bedrooms and baths are on the first level, opening towards the courtyard. The second level comprises the living/dining area, with a courtyard between the interior and the view. A shutter makes it possible to transform a small but intimate courtyard into a terrace with a view. Service areas and the staircase are all placed above each other at the rear of the cube.

John Pawson
London

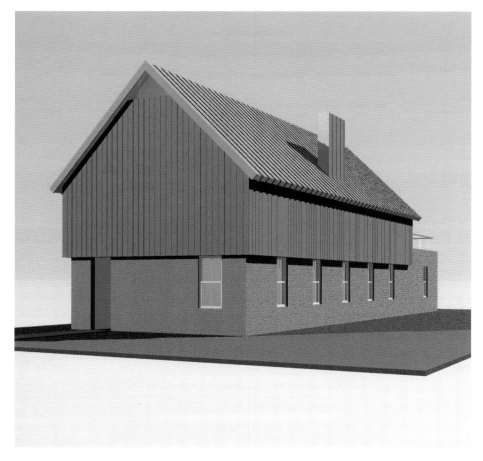

Central to the design of this house in the ski resort town of Telluride, Colorado – once an old mining settlement in the Rockies – is its urban context. While the scheme is in no way a Victorian pastiche, it does look to the vernacular building forms developed by the pioneers to protect themselves from the extremes of the Colorado winters.

The house is on two floors, although it appears to be smaller: with windows on the flank wall on the ground floor only, the second floor appears to be hidden. The roof is pitched, maintaining the historic scale of Telluride's buildings. By keeping to the east side of the building plot, the house maintains and enhances existing views. Public rooms are on the upper floor, to take advantage of the mountain views through glazed gable ends, while bedrooms and bathrooms are on the ground floor.

Materials reflect the local palette with stone flank walls, a timber upper structure and a metal roof. The house is in a protected wetland, and landscaping will recognize and enhance its fragile ecosystem.

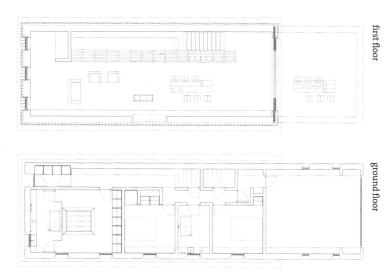

first floor

ground floor

Walsh house, Telluride
Colorado, USA

Architect
John Pawson

Construction
1998–99

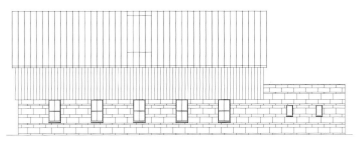 

Pichler & Traupmann
Vienna

Drexler house
Pinkafeld, Austria

Christoph Pichler and
Hannes Traupmann

Construction
1995–97

The Drexler house is a response to
the surrounding landscape, not just
in the location of terraces and
entrances, but even in the specific
characteristics of individual rooms.
The high and enclosed entrance,
for example, is a paraphrase of a
small canon with which it is aligned.

A visually 'heavy' concrete upper
part, which sits on a seemingly
lighter white base are the two main
elements to dominate the building.
The white plastered base of the
building contains the entrance, plus
the cooking, dining and living areas,
and includes the outdoor pool. From
this base, a concrete sculpture in the
form of a continuous sheet unfolds
into a complex architectural
structure, containing the bedrooms
and bathroom.

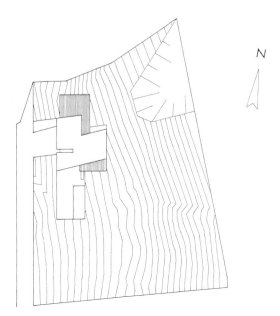

Buchholz-Ost
Berlin, Germany

Project team
Helmut Richter with
Ahmet Alata

Design
1997

Helmut Richter
Vienna

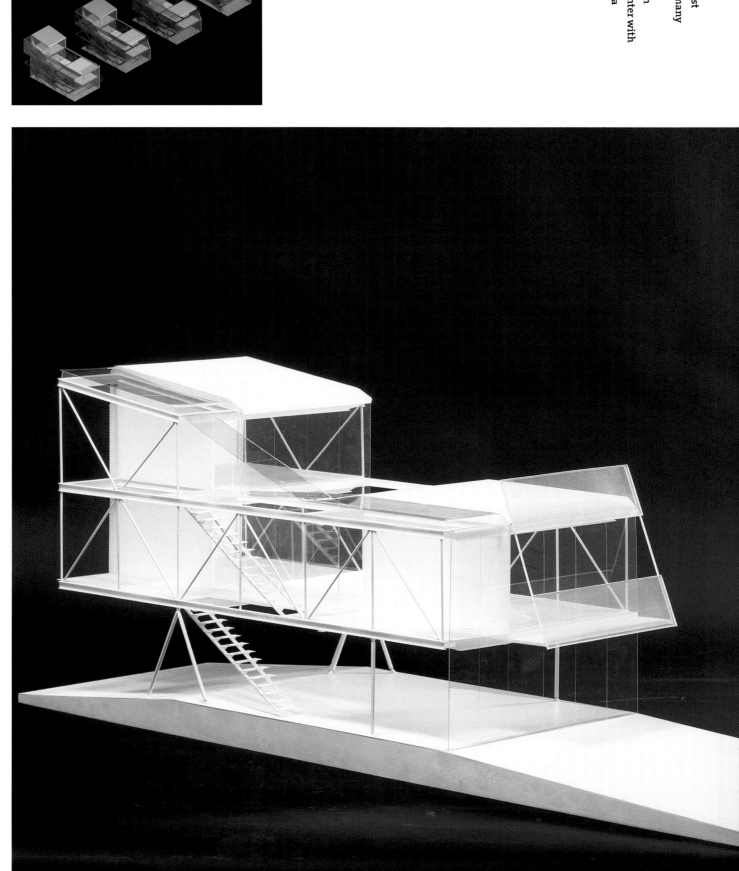

For the Berlin 1999 building exhibition, Helmut Richter has developed a house typology that can be modified to respond to specific contextual conditions. A steel construction system clad in sandwich panels keeps the interior free of any structural partitions. Six different house types can be created from the same structural system, which offers privacy from the gaze of neighbours in the high-density setting. Each house has a roofed carport and garden. Closed on the north and east sides in most cases, the houses open up to the south and west, using the sun as passive energy. The houses have two to three floors, the general width of each type being 7.23 metres (23 feet); the length, depending on the type, is between 14.37 metres (47 feet), 12.53 metres (41 feet) and 9.57 metres (31 feet).

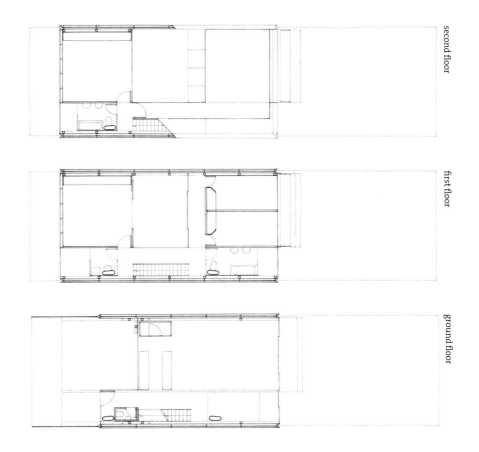

second floor

first floor

ground floor

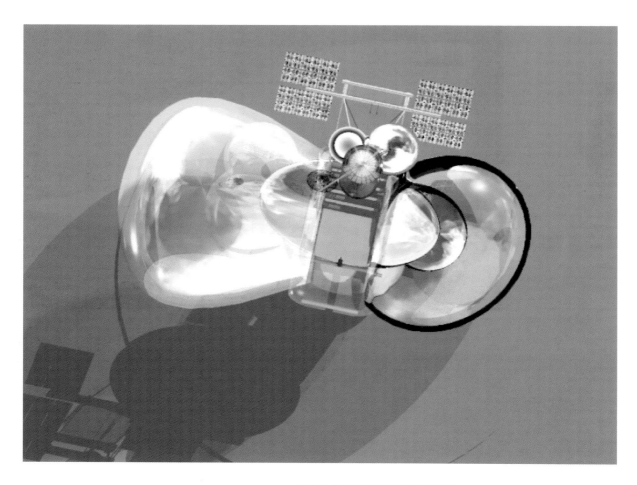

The brief was to design a modern *Kolonihaven* – a short-stay living/recreational scheme based on the original nineteenth-century model. The houses will be built for the year 2000 as part of the City of Copenhagen's millennium celebrations. The design is for an adaptive, relocateable short-stay living enclosure that could potentially change from hour to hour, from day to night, utilizing a simple light-weight architectural form. The building is designed to be able to adapt to the site's changing daily and seasonal characteristics whilst registering the needs of individuals.

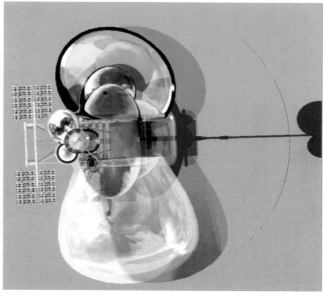

Richard Rogers Partnership
London

Kolonihaven
Copenhagen, Denmark

Project team
Richard Rogers,
Mike Davies, Marco
Goldschmied,
John Young
with Jenny Jones,
Harvinder Gabhari,
Maurice Brennan

Client
Jointly Museum
of Modern Art/
Royal Academy
in Copenhagen

Construction
1996–99

The Bachelor house
Minneapolis, Minnesota, USA

Project team
Joel Sanders with Charles Stone,
Claes Appelquist,
Nicholas Haagensen,
Cedric Cornu,
Mark Tsurumaki,
Alexandra Ultsch

Design and construction
1997–99

Joel Sanders
New York

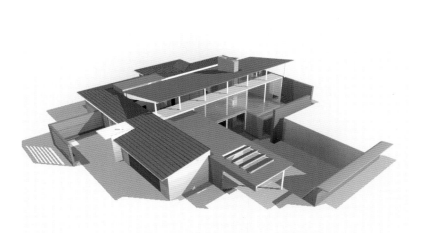

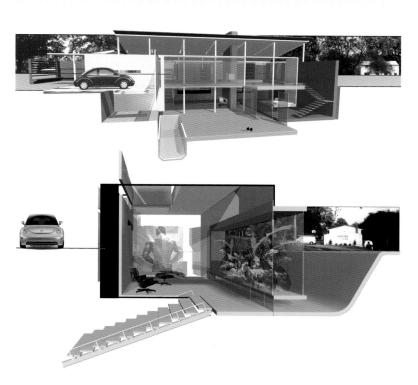

The Bachelor house responds to the gap between the domestic requirements of the traditional nuclear family – as typically accommodated within the American suburban house – and the lifestyle of the contemporary bachelor, a person with no intention of marrying or procreating. Located in a suburban neighbourhood just minutes from downtown Minneapolis, the design – literally built upon the foundations of a 1950s 'Rambler' – retains the existing facade and uses it like a mask to conceal the surprisingly unorthodox construction behind.

Tailored to the bachelor's conflicting desires for openness to the outdoors and privacy from neighbours, the architects have excavated rather than built up. An Astroturf fence raises the level of the horizon at one end, blocking out views of neighbouring houses, and slopes down into the subterranean basement/backyard at the other, forming a soft ground plane where the bachelor can exercise and lounge by the indoor pool. The house is made of a wood frame and brick veneer construction, steel-pipe columns and an aluminium and glass curtain wall.

Responding to the specific household needs of the professional bachelor living here, the design eliminates the compartmentalized rooms of the conventional suburban dwelling in favour of the open kitchen, dining and living area, den and study located above, and a master bedroom suite and spa placed adjacent to the underground backyard below.

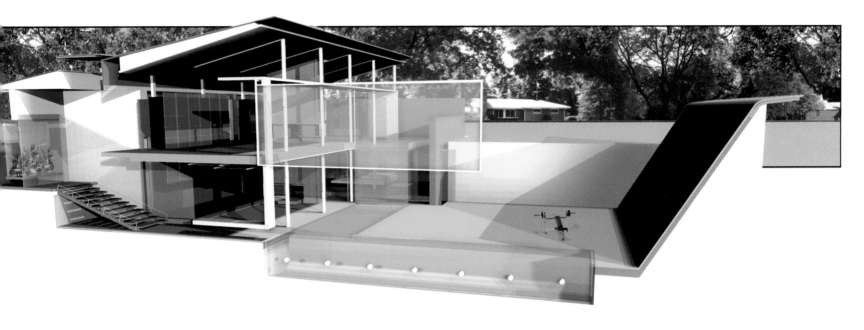

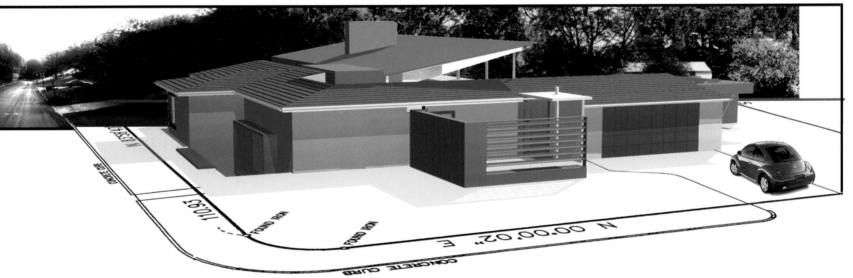

The n-house
West London, UK

Matthias Sauerbruch
and Louisa Hutton

Project team
Matthias Sauerbruch,
Louisa Hutton with
Andrew Llowarch
(project architect),
Dinka Izetbegovic (drawings)

Construction
1997–99

Sauerbruch Hutton Architects
London/Berlin

A six-storey listed Victorian house in a west London terrace, formerly a hotel, has been reconstructed to create a family dwelling. The house is read as a sequence of spatial volumes, defined from the inside by the enclosing surfaces of the historic architecture, complete with cornices, architraves and skirtings. Each of these spaces is redefined by means of a new mat which is laid over its floor surface. The selection of materials for the mats – hardwood and stone, through to rubber, screed, gravel, carpet and leather – reflects the social and spatial hierarchy of the rooms. A series of contemporary objects inhabit the newly defined spaces of the house, carriers of the paraphernalia necessary for everyday life. The ordering of these pieces – in terms of their number and frequency – complements that of the historic fabric, whose presence in the house decreases as one progresses up from the ground floor and the 'piano nobile' through to the upper floors.

Within the historic spaces, the furniture inserts tend to be large free-standing objects, with rich and contrasting textures and materials – rubber, concrete, hardwood, steel and lacquer – which together create a focused intensity within the existing language of the house. Elsewhere, the furniture insertions consist of large-scale, space-making elements, characterized by an intensity of colour that tends to dematerialize the elements and allows them to be experienced primarily as phenomena and secondly as object. In addition, there are smaller pieces that cluster on the boundaries of the space.

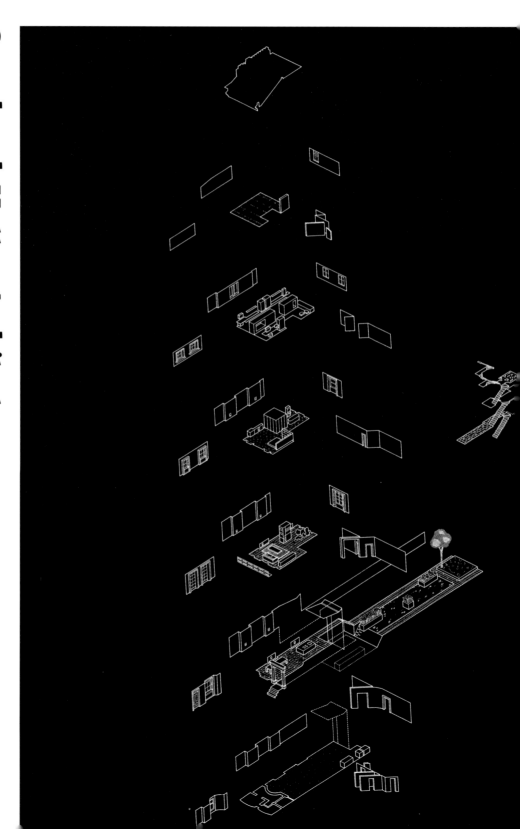

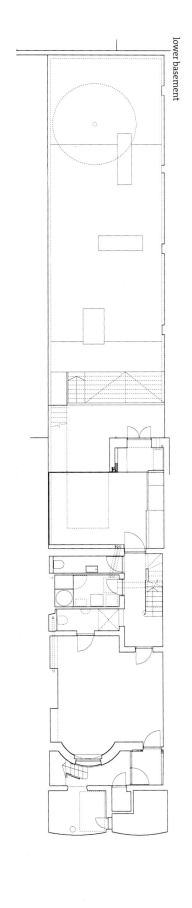

lower basement

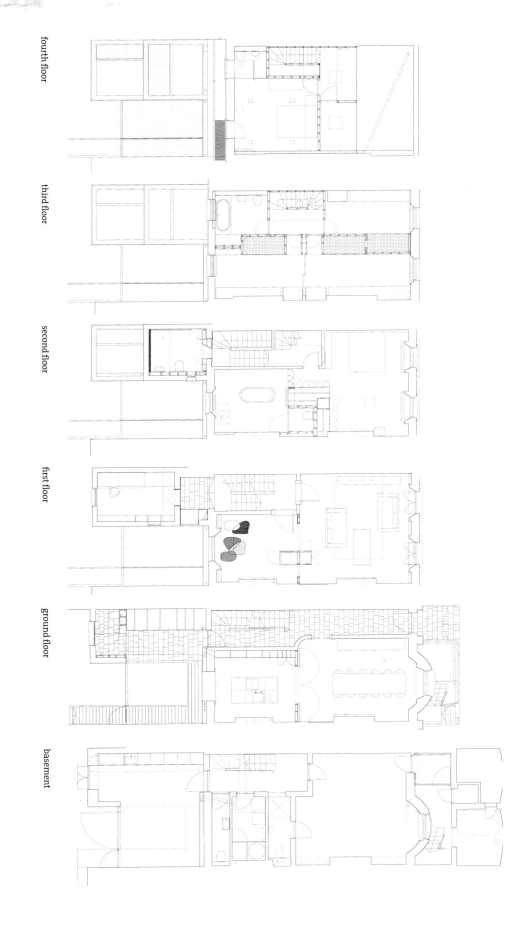

fourth floor

third floor

second floor

first floor

ground floor

basement

Located in Beverly Hills, California, Smith-Miller + Hawkinson's addition to an addition is a house for an increasingly successful and therefore increasingly wealthy film producer. The original structure was a Case Study house designed by Donald Polsky in the early 1950s. The Shaye residence addition was designed by Smith-Miller + Hawkinson in the early 1980s. The latest house has been designed without using programmatic elements from either the original statement of modernism, nor the architects' own later design. Instead, the existing buildings are contrasted, promoting ideas of occupation in an area that has very tight building restrictions.

The ideas of exterior and interior have been diffused through rolling and sliding doors, consequently providing more space than the law actually permits. These invisible laws and regulations – which had originally made this project unfeasible – together with the client's brief, have defined a series of seemingly casually linked buildings. The plan configuration suggests the entry of the building through an open-air garage (carport) instead of the traditional front door and includes a large-format screening room, a guest suite, a second-storey private office, several different parking spaces and a painting studio.

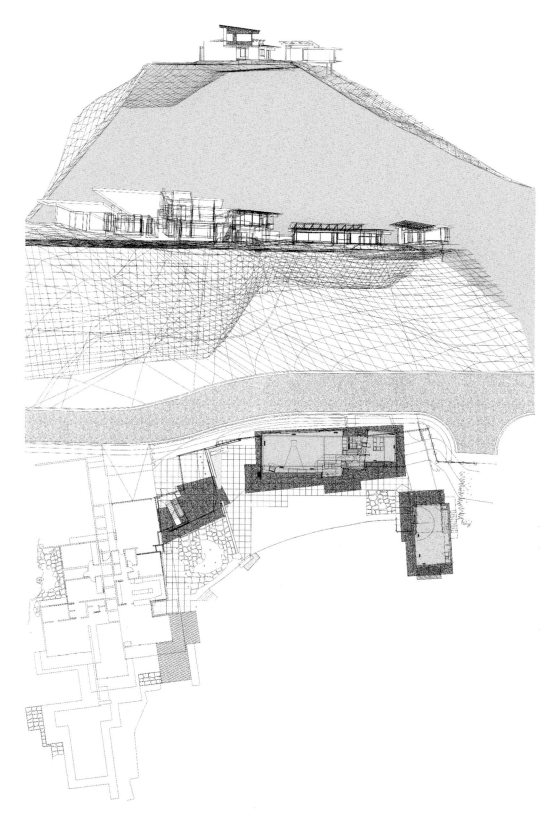

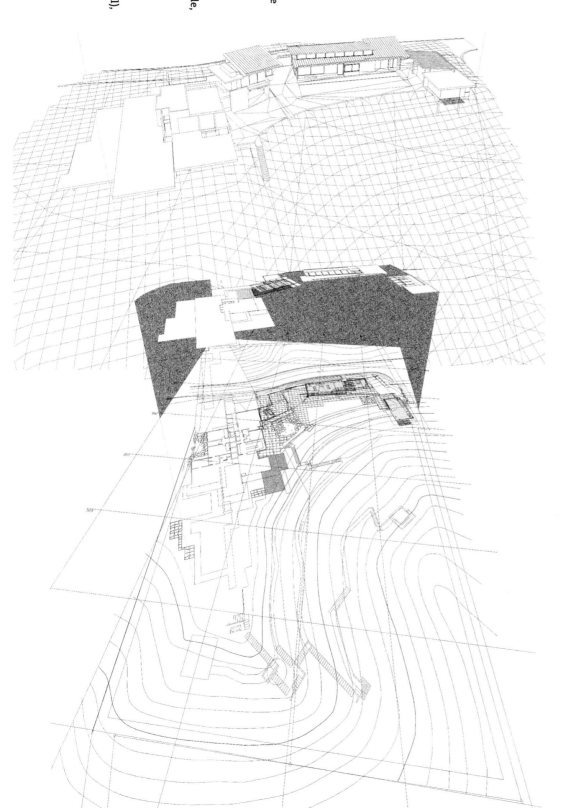

Smith-Miller + Hawkinson Architects
New York

Shaye residence:
addition to an addition
Los Angeles, California, USA

Henry Smith-Miller and
Laurie Hawkinson

Project team
Henry Smith-Miller, Laurie
Hawkinson with Starling Keene
(project architect),
Alexis Kraft (project manager),
Margi Glagovic Nothard
(concept design),
Ferda Kolatan, Keith Krumwiede,
Oliver Lang, Christian Lynch
(design team),
Steven Mezey & Associates
(structural),
Helman/Haloosim (mechanical),
Achva Benzinberg Stein
(landscape),
Archetype (contractor)

Construction
1995–98

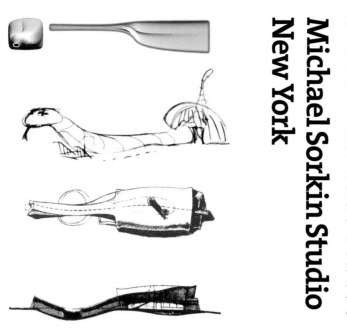

Michael Sorkin Studio
New York

Partly a master plan for the transformation of an ex-commune into housing with broad scope for appeal, the Herd houses are designed to join existing apartment buildings, new lofts and single-house building plots, in order to increase the diversity of the site. Each of the Herd houses – though based on a repetitive envelope – is to be configured to the special needs of its occupants: a ground-floor space for example can become a garage, workshop, bedroom, shop or social space. And retaining something of the original communal vibe, the houses – with their accessible roofs and cross-cutting circulation – will weave public and private uses together in new ways.

Herd houses
Friedrichshof, Austria

Project team
Michael Sorkin
with Andrei Vovk,
Mitchell Joachim,
Victoria Marshall

Construction
1998–99

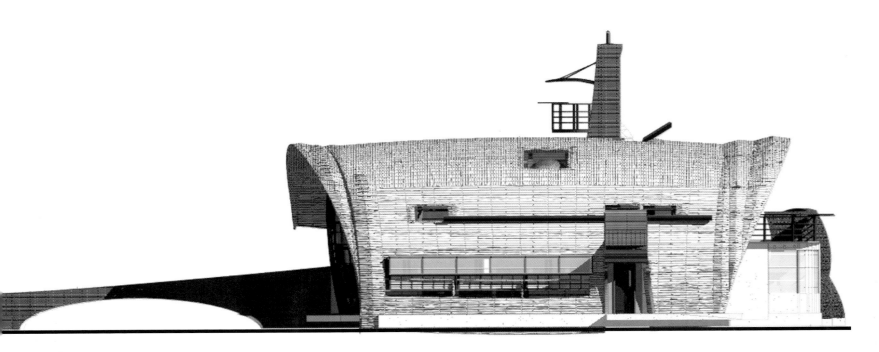

Nanon house
Lanaken, Belgium

Project team
Ettore Sottsass,
Johanna Grawunder
with Oliver Layseca
(project architect),
Norbert Forster
(associated architect)

Construction
1995–98

The Nanon house is situated on a large, flat piece of land surrounded by tall trees. It is organized into a family area of 800 square metres (8,600 square feet), with three bedrooms, a kitchen, dining area, living room and study with a large central courtyard and physical training area of 500 square metres (5,380 square feet) consisting of an indoor pool, sauna/steambath and exercise rooms. Architecturally, the project is conceived as more like a village with its expressed volumes and voids, than a single building.

floor plan

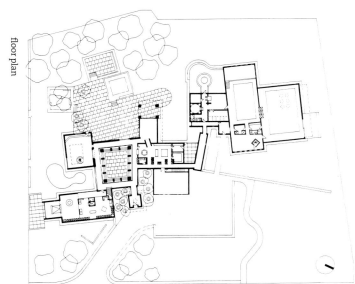

'A group of friends working for an intimidating client. An old mansion in the hills of Maresme, a beautiful coastline, north of Barcelona. A mansion with remaining traces of its seventeenth-century origins that has been regularly adapted and extended, culminating in a major rebuilding in 1900. A very beautiful, generous site, sloping down towards the sea, with a forest of pine trees, oak, cypresses, olive trees, and other Mediterranean plants, a place in which to create a fascinating garden.

'A daring client who believes in us. I hope this occasion will bring us enlightenment, diversity and the joy of a successful outcome.' Oscar Tusquets

Tusquets, Diaz & Associades
Barcelona

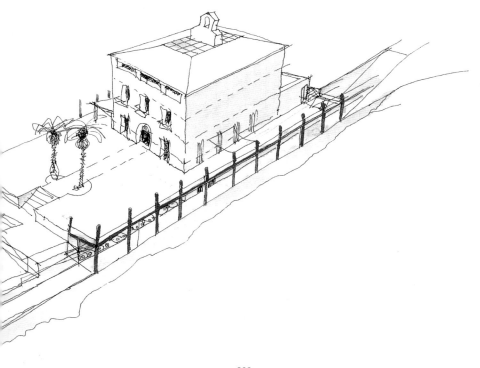

Can Misser
Barcelona, Spain

Oscar Tusquets

Project team
Oscar Tusquets with Carles Diaz,
Carles Vinardell, Maria Roger
(project architect),
Enric Torrent
(structural architect),
Pierre Arnaud (exterior lighting),
Ingo Maurer (interior lighting),
Jesús Jiménez (engineer),
Pere Valldepérez (glazier),
Bet Figueras (landscape),
Sunchi Echegaray
(interior furnishings),
Jaume Tresserra
(furniture design),
Naxo Farreras (model),
Lluís Casals (model photography)

Construction
1998–99

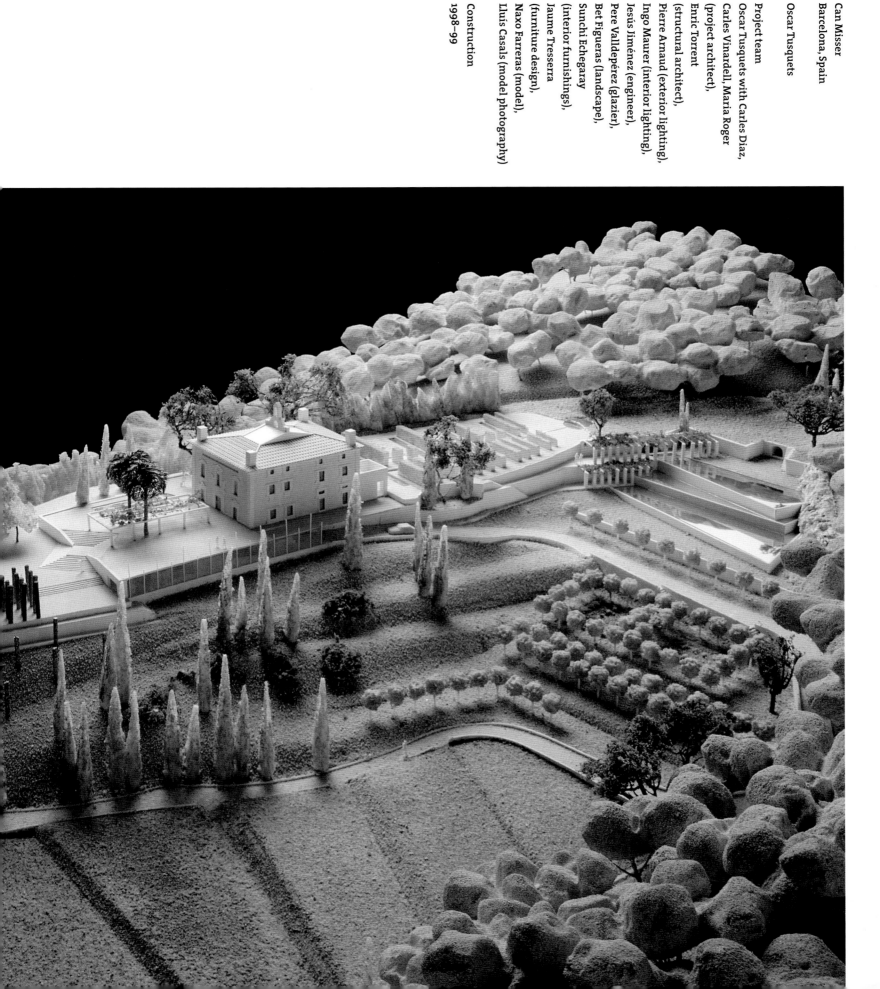

Ulla and Lasse Vahtera
Oulu

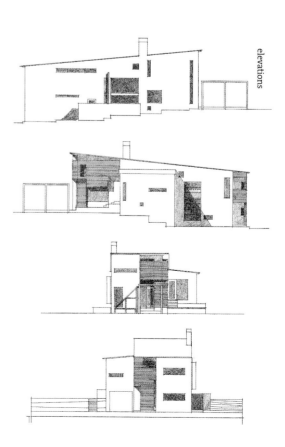

elevations

The Laitinen house was
commissioned by two scientists,
with two sons, aged nine and
seventeen. The starting point for
the design was not so much the site
itself – a private plot of land near
the Oulu river – as the taste and
personality of the family: the client's
rational, scientific disposition
indicated a design based on the
cool and functional use of materials
and colours.

The site slopes northwards and
to the street and is surrounded by
high birch trees. The house is a
simple white box, clad in plywood
at the rear. A south-facing courtyard
offers an intimate, sheltered outdoor
living room.

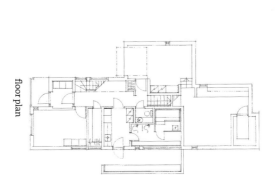

floor plan

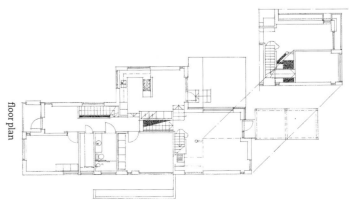

floor plan

235

Michael Wilford
London

House in Sussex
Sussex, UK

Project team
Michael Wilford
with Suzanne Garrett
and David Guy,
Whitby Bird and Partners
(structural and
mechanical engineering),
Martin Osborn (contractor)

Construction
1996–99

ground floor

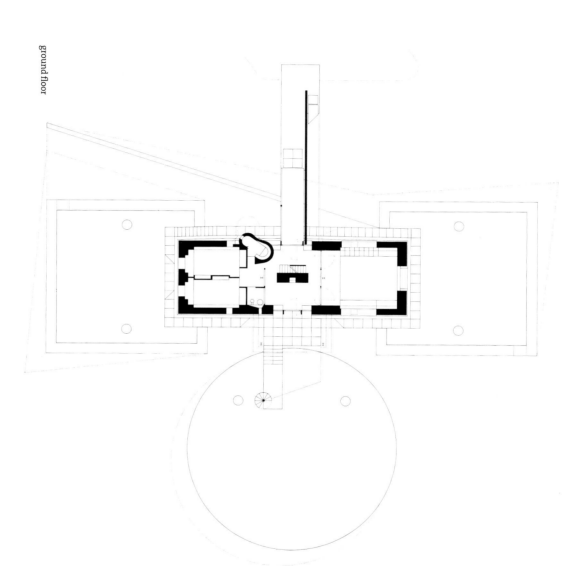

cross section

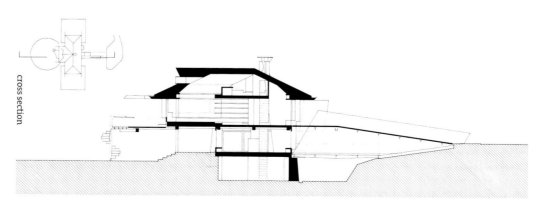

236

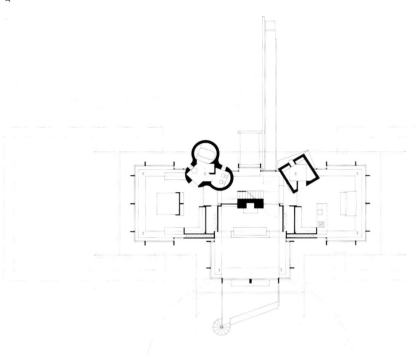

This design balances a sensitive response to a rural environment with provision of facilities for modern living. It combines the indigenous materials of sandstone and timber with plate glass and stainless steel in a collage of traditional building techniques and modern architectural ideas.

The terrain slopes diagonally from the south-east corner, and the approach unfolds in a sequence encompassing the whole property. A hedge lining the circular drive conceals the house until arrival at the point of entry at the top of the site. The house, together with the flat, geometric 'outdoor rooms' extending from it, forms a counterpoint to the inclined natural landscape. Primary living spaces are located at the first-floor level and enjoy extensive heath and forest views. Square living, kitchen/dining and master bedrooms cluster around the upper entrance hall and the central chimney/stair core, beneath an all-embracing shallow-pitched roof. The inner area of the split-level living room forms a snug around an open fireplace while the outer zone opens, through sliding windows, on to a balcony connected by a spiral stair to the circular lawn below. A mezzanine above the snug overlooks the living room and entrance hall. The rectangular stone base contains guest rooms and a plunge pool on either side of the ground-floor entrance lobby, above basement service spaces. The trefoil and entrance bridge establish a vertical order in contrast to the overall horizontal form of the house. Spaces, forms and materials expand, contract and interlock with each other within and through the building envelope.

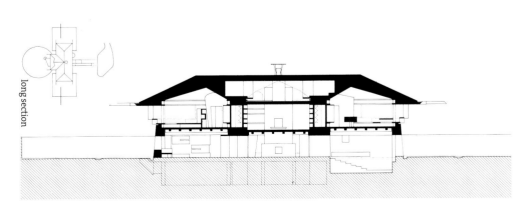

Index

Credits